THE FOUR
COMMITMENTS
OF A WINNING TEAM

THE FOUR
COMMITMENTS
OF A WINNING TEAM

MARK EATON

GREENLEAF
BOOK GROUP PRESS

Published by Greenleaf Book Group Press
Austin, Texas
www.gbgpress.com

Distributed by Greenleaf Book Group

For ordering information or special discounts for bulk purchases, please contact Greenleaf Book Group at PO Box 91869, Austin, TX 78709, 512.891.6100.

Design and composition by Francine Platt, Eden Graphics, Inc.
Cover design by Shekhar Patil and Francine Platt, Eden Graphics, Inc.
Front cover photo by Dirk Douglas
Back cover photo by Tim de Frisco /Allsport / Getty Images

Publisher's Cataloging-in-Publication data is available.

Print ISBN: 978-1-62634-532-4

eBook ISBN: 978-1-62634-533-l

Part of the Tree Neutral® program, which offsets the number of trees consumed in the production and printing of this book by taking proactive steps, such as planting trees in direct proportion to the number of trees used: www.treeneutral.com

Printed in the United States of America on acid-free paper

18 19 20 21 22 23   10 9 8 7 6 5 4 3 2 1

First Edition

To Coach Tom Lubin,
who believed in me and dared
to dream big.

TABLE OF CONTENTS

"UNTIL ONE IS *COMMITTED*, there is hesitancy, the chance to draw back, always ineffectiveness. Concerning all acts of initiative (and creation), there is one elementary truth, the ignorance of which kills countless ideas and splendid plans: that the moment one definitely commits oneself, then Providence moves too.

All sorts of things occur to help one that would never otherwise have occurred. A whole stream of events issues from the decision, raising in one's favour all manner of unforeseen incidents and meetings and material assistance, which no man could have dreamt would have come his way. I have learned a deep respect for one of Goethe's couplets:

Whatever you can do, or dream you can, begin it. Boldness has genius, power, and magic in it!"

– WILLIAM HUTCHINSON MURRAY
The Scottish Himalayan Expedition (1951)

FOREWORD

I MET MARK EATON in the summer of 1984. I had recently been drafted by the Utah Jazz and was invited to a banquet in Salt Lake City where the team was celebrating their Midwest Division Championship, the first in franchise history. I knew very little about the NBA, and even less about the Utah Jazz. I arrived in town all eyes and ears. I didn't have the foggiest notion what to expect, especially since the locals had booed my selection at the draft a month earlier. Almost immediately this mountain of a man, who I recognized as Mark Eaton, walked toward me. I had been around big people my whole life, but this guy blocked out the sun! I guess I expected him to be bashful about his size, slightly stooped, or a little awkward. But he was none of those things. I also thought the league's leading shot blocker would simply shake hands and move on.

Within moments, I found out how wrong I was. Mark greeted me with warmth and grace. If he had doubts about me, or the merits of the Jazz's choice, he didn't show it. I am certain he had never seen me bounce a ball, yet he welcomed me as if we had already shared a nine-year career and were life-long friends. Our meeting seemed more like a reunion than an introduction. Standing tall, he exuded confidence and intelligence. There was a lot more to this guy than a 7'4" frame. I liked him immediately.

That day Salt Lake City honored a team that accomplished one of the most difficult things in all of sports: They changed the culture of a franchise from losers to winners. It was no fluke. From that point forward, the Utah Jazz strung together a record twenty consecutive winning seasons and playoff appearances. Mark was a key to that success. All of us who followed were able to build on what that team and coaching staff had done. They had learned how to win and we would be the beneficiaries.

Mark is one of the very best teammates I ever had. He understood he would need every edge when facing the likes of Kareem Abdul-Jabbar, Ralph Sampson, and Hakeem Olajuwon. He was prepared for every practice. His preparation wasn't limited to watching film, scanning scouting reports, or making extra hook shots after practice; it was broader than that. He researched techniques that would help keep his body tuned up. He consumed foods that fueled his body and mind. He recognized the importance of getting enough sleep and developed a routine to ensure he was well rested. In short, he was the consummate professional who sought out every conceivable way within his control to give his team a chance to win.

Mark and I spent a lot of time together over the course of our careers. He was fun to talk to and a pleasure to be around. From our first road trip my rookie season to the last playoff game we played together, he would knock on my hotel door and say, "Come on, let's go eat." We ate most of our meals together. He was great company, but boy did he draw attention in every restaurant from sea to shining sea. People would gawk and make comments, out loud, as though Mark couldn't hear them. I wonder how many times I heard "Oh my *God!*" or "How is the weather up there?" One time I just couldn't take it any more. After watching people stare, point, laugh, and make an obnoxious observation, I snapped. I began barking out a heated little lesson on manners and courtesy when Mark set his hand on my shoulder and said, "It's okay Stocks; let it go. I'm used to it." And he was! While I simmered through my cheeseburger, he enjoyed his nice nutritious meal and the rest of the evening without letting the intrusive comments get to him.

As I read Mark's book, *The Four Commitments of a Winning Team*, it occurred to me that he practices what he preaches—and always has. Preparation and commitment to excellence were the cornerstones of his basketball career, and this book is another example of both. The last of his Four Commitments is "Protect Others," and he made a life in the NBA doing just that. Mark took care of his teammates on the court and off. That, in large part, is why we were successful and why he continues to be successful. As you might suspect, this book is an interesting and worthwhile read and I highly recommend it.

Mark Eaton is a man that you would want in a foxhole with you when all heck breaks loose. You can count on him, every day, all day. He took me under his wing thirty-four years ago and has never wavered in his commitment to me in any way. I am honored to be included as one of his friends.

– John Stockton

INTRODUCTION

E VERYONE LOVES a winning team. Everyone wants to be on a winning team. Yet teamwork seems to have taken a backseat to individual achievement. Today solo stats are lauded, and individual performance is highlighted and celebrated at the expense of teamwork and unity. This trend has caused a decline in team functionality in all sectors of society, from the basketball court and football field to the factory floor and boardroom.

I know from experience, however, that teamwork and individual recognition can, and should, co-exist.

I had the immense good fortune to be a key member of the Utah Jazz for twelve seasons. I did not ascend to my position among some of basketball's biggest stars in any of the usual ways. My journey from auto mechanic to NBA All-Star was not only unique, it was somewhat miraculous. On this journey, I discovered the Four Commitments, life lessons gleaned from mentors; these Commitments carried me to unprecedented heights in sports and business. They led me to an NBA record, two NBA Defensive Player of the Year titles, a position on an All-Star team, a successful speaking career, and prosperous entrepreneurial ventures.

In this book, I will share the Four Commitments with

you and show you how to incorporate them in a way that will not just elevate your individual performance but will help you to understand your role as a team player in new and wide-ranging ways. These tenets will give you a winning advantage and increase your team's productivity and success. In addition, as you integrate the Commitments into your life, you will inspire your co-workers, family, and teammates in ways that will propel them forward as well.

In developing the Four Commitments, I became intensely aware of how connected we all are. What we do and how we do it has a powerful impact on the success of those around us. The way our teammates function has a direct bearing on our experience and success as well. *We are all in this game of life together!* Realizing this intensified my desire to assist others and to share the lessons I learned when I employed the Four Commitments on the basketball court, in the boardroom, and on the speaking circuit.

In this book, I will take you on the journey of how I learned and applied each of the following Commitments and how you can do the same:

COMMITMENT #1 – Know Your Job

COMMITMENT #2 – Do What You're Asked To Do

COMMITMENT #3 – Make People Look Good

COMMITMENT #4 – Protect Others

When you embrace the Four Commitments you will clearly establish your position and responsibilities within your team, and move forward with clarity and focus toward your common goals. People flourish and companies grow when we collaborate, share, and work together. When we are committed to each other and honor our connection, we form winning teams. And when our team wins, we win.

CHAPTER 1

"Commitment separates those who live their
dreams from those who live their lives regretting
the opportunities they have squandered."

— BILL RUSSELL

I T'S SUNDAY, FEBRUARY 12, 1989, and I'm standing at half
court in the Houston Astrodome. Forty-five thousand
screaming fans crowd the arena, their combined voices
deafening. Over 200 million fans will watch this game live
on worldwide TV.

The announcer's voice booms through the speakers like
the voice of God, sending chills down my spine: "And now,
introducing your Western Conference All-Stars."

My teammates Karl Malone and John Stockton stand to
my left. To my right are Kareem Abdul-Jabbar and Hakeem
Olajuwon. Across from me Michael Jordan, Charles
Barkley, Dominique Wilkins, Moses Malone, and Kevin
McHale make up an imposing squad of giants. These *are*
the biggest names in basketball. I watch the crowd and listen as they roar from the upper deck and I feel small—a
feeling that I, at 7'4", am not too familiar with. The reality
of where I am settles in.

The noise in the arena intensifies. "From the Portland Trailblazers, Clyde Drexler!" "From the Los Angeles Lakers, James Worthy!" The fans shout their approval. They are so loud I feel the vibration of the court beneath me.

On the bus ride to the stadium, I had looked at my fellow players, struck by the talent seated around me. All world-class athletes, some of them had played in fifteen All-Star games! I wondered if this felt normal to them or if this wasn't a big deal.

It was a big deal to me.

These were the top basketball players in the world, and I was one of them. This was the ultimate honor: to be selected as one of the best in a profession. Nothing could possibly match this feeling. I can't believe I'm here. The reverberating sound from the Astrodome fades, and in my mind's eye, I see myself as a sixteen-year-old kid, sitting on the bench at Westminster High School in Southern California.

I'm wearing my sweats. There is no point in taking them off. I know the coach won't put me in the game—he never does. I try to remain focused on the play. I watch as our guard, Tony Engedal, takes the ball down the court and nails another basket. I feel disconnected from the crowd who throw their support and enthusiasm behind our team as they score bucket after bucket, putting us up by 25 points.

I glance up the bench just as Coach Ferguson gives me the look. I can see the wheels turning: He thinks our lead is big enough to risk putting me in the game. He gives me a nod, and I hurry to pull off my sweats. I head to the scorer's table to check in and hustle onto the floor. I glimpse my mom in the stands. She is always there, even though I rarely get playing time. I feel a moment of relief that my dad is busy working and can't be at the game. The earsplitting sound of the buzzer prompts me into motion. I take a deep breath and head onto the court. *Do something right, Mark! Don't choke.*

No sooner do I reach the court than a player from Marina High School steals the ball from our guard and transitions into a fast break, running up the court and moving into position to score. Players sprint past me to the other end of the court in a blur of uniforms. The coach screams, "Get back, Mark!" The words resonate in my head, but their guard is a foot shorter than I am, and ten times faster. He drives in for an easy lay-up just as I reach the free throw line. I feel every eye in the gym on me. I know what they're thinking: *He's 6'11"! Why isn't he dominating?* I wonder the same thing.

The Astrodome announcer's voice explodes through the microphone and pulls me back to the electric atmosphere of the All-Star game. "And now, at 7'4", 290 pounds, the NBA leader in blocked shots, from the Utah Jazz, making his All-Star debut, Number 53, center, Mark Eaton!"

Time freezes. The sound is thunderous, the spotlight blinding. I smile, hold up my hand, and wave.

"And those are your 1989 NBA All-Stars!"

I glance up at the scoreboard: It reads double zeros on both sides with twelve minutes on the clock. The crowd settles in as the starters make their way to center court. The ball is tossed up; Olajuwon taps it out to Alex English.

English makes a cross-court pass to Dale Ellis, who slams it home with a two handed dunk. I sit forward on the bench and cheer on my team. It was not so long ago that the bench had a very different feeling.

It was the start of my senior year at UCLA. My skills had improved and I was ready to play. Coach Farmer, however, doesn't know what to do with me. To him, I'm a 7'4" question mark on a team he's struggling to bring back to prominence in his debut season as head coach.

It's the bench and me again. Even though I work my tail off at practice. Even though I arrive at the gym earlier than my teammates and leave later. Even though I helped take my junior college team to the state championship, I'm on the bench. *This is ridiculous. How am I supposed to get drafted into the NBA when I only play three minutes a game?*

It's a Wednesday afternoon, four thirty, as practice wraps up at Pauley Pavilion and we head to the locker room. Tomorrow we board a plane and prepare to play two PAC-10 rivals, Oregon and Oregon State. I put it all out there on the court today in hopes Coach would see something to inspire him to give me more time in a game. After all, it is the last road trip of the season and the end of my playing career at UCLA. I am looking forward to this trip. As I sit down to take off my shoes, Coach Farmer asks me to step into his office.

"Hey, Mark," he said. "I just wanted to let you know that, uh, we won't need you in the Oregon series this weekend."

"I'm sorry. What did you say?"

"Just that, you know, we only have room for twelve

players when we travel and we've decided to take a freshman with us. We are not taking you on the trip. I'm sure you understand."

My face turns warm, then flaming hot. *Understand? No, I definitely do not understand why I will miss the last series of my senior year!*

I make a beeline for the double doors. The lights are out, the gym dark. I grab the nearest thing I can find, a metal trash can lid, and hurl it as hard as I can. It crashes onto the court, skids, and rolls until it smacks against a wall, falls into a slow spin, and is silent.

As it lands, I hear the sound of my dreams being crushed.

I have given everything to this game, to this team. I know I can contribute. I saw it when I played at Cypress Junior College before being recruited by UCLA. Why won't these coaches give me a chance? What if this is it for me? What if I'm not going pro?

The jubilant cheering of the crowd brings me back to the action in Houston. The game is in full swing. Coach Pat Riley looks down the bench and motions to me. I pull off my sweats and head to the scorer's table. The horn sounds. I signal to Kareem Abdul-Jabbar as I sub in, and he gives me a nod as we pass.

Charles Barkley is shooting free throws, and I take my place under the basket. I can't help but look at the crowd and wonder, how the hell did I get here? How did a bench-warmer from Westminster High School become an NBA All-Star?

Professional sports teams provide a spotlight for the world's top athletes. In the National Football League there are about 1,500 players, and there are nearly 900 players in Major League Baseball. The National Basketball Association is small by comparison with approximately 400 players at any given time—the elite of the elite.

I realize how fortunate I was to be among those 400, especially considering my career nearly ended before it began. For more than a decade, I played with a great team against the best players in NBA history. I witnessed first-hand that success is not guaranteed, even when the very best athletes play for the very best coaches. There are teams and players who struggle year after year, and those who excel. I know what the difference is. It is a simple but pro-found truth. Teamwork.

From every minute on the court, every speech in the locker room, every second of practice and training, I learned the transformative power of teamwork.

Retiring after an incredible career and twelve seasons with the Utah Jazz, I have continued to experience the transformative power of teamwork off the court. Using the Four Commitments of teamwork I learned from play-ing basketball, I have successfully started and run several businesses, worked closely with dozens of the nation's top business leaders, and delivered hundreds of presentations to the country's foremost companies and organizations.

Through all this, I have repeatedly seen the Four Com-mitments contribute to individual and institutional success. The results of teamwork—the willingness to work alongside others and develop a deep, synergistic rapport—invariably exceed people's greatest expectations. Conversely, I have seen the toll a lack of those same fundamentals can take on a team and its members.

Teamwork is often misunderstood. Countless people talk about it, but few truly understand it. Teamwork is something one assumes is *automatically* in place when one joins a team. However, the true fundamentals of teamwork are more than a mindset. They are more than the idea of working together. *A team is a group of people who commit to each other.* When that commitment happens, your team will be a united, unstoppable force.

Though many people hold the opinion that athletes are selfish, my years in the NBA taught me there was no room to be self-centered. With 20,000 fans in the arena focused on you, and millions more watching on TV, there is too much at stake not to collaborate and cooperate.

In the pages that follow, I will share the vital fundamentals of teamwork that have fueled my own success, and that of the teams and companies that I work with. I have used these to become a successful speaker, business owner, author, and community leader. Now, I share these commitments with you, distilled in a philosophy so simple, you can implement them today and see results tomorrow.

CHAPTER 2

"Good things take time, as they should. We shouldn't expect good things to happen overnight. Actually, getting something too easily or too soon can cheapen the outcome."

- JOHN WOODEN

MY NBA CAREER had a much less auspicious start than one might imagine. My big break came in, of all places, a tire store. Specifically the Mark C. Bloome tire store, where I worked as an auto mechanic.

I was in Orange County, California, made good money, and hung out with my friends. On top of that, I was able to get out to the docks some nights to help my dad. He taught a diesel mechanics class at Long Beach City College, but in the evening he liked to make a little extra money fixing boats. I liked the time with him.

It was a typical day at work. I liked the pace and the variety of tasks I was assigned. The year I spent after high school, working my way through trade school in Arizona, had paid off. My boss had promoted me from mounting tires to tune-ups, shocks, oil changes, and brakes.

I was content, and unaware my life was about to change dramatically.

I had just waved good-bye to a customer when a car screeched into the parking lot and nearly clipped me. Mark C. Bloome was located at one of the busiest intersections in Buena Park, so we were used to drive-up customers. The driver jumped out and ran over to me with such purpose I thought his engine had to be on fire at the very least.

"Hi!"

"Uh hi, sir, is everything okay? How can I help you?"

"I was just driving by and noticed ..."

Please tell me this is about his car.

"You're tall!"

Here we go again.

"Yep."

"Really tall!"

"Yes sir, 7'4"."

"I was just wondering if, uh ..."

Don't ask. Please don't ask.

"Do you play basketball?"

I suppose it is an inevitable question when you stand head and shoulders above everyone. It does not mean, however, that I liked the intrusion. I was constantly barraged with very personal questions and expected to respond to absolute strangers or be judged as rude and aloof. At the grocery store, people asked me to reach things off the top shelf, while they sputtered on about how great I must be at basketball. Old men stopped me at the gas station and hammered me with questions about my height, and that of my parents and siblings. Everywhere I went I was on display.

"You've gotta play basketball, right?" the man continued as he paced in the parking lot.

"No, I don't. Now if you need a tune-up or an oil change, I'd be happy to help you."

"I just can't believe you don't play ball. You had to play in high school, right? Any college ball?"

I ignored his questions, let him know that the employees at Mark C. Bloome would be happy to help him with his future auto needs, and walked back in the shop.

Two days later, as I was finishing rebuilding a carburetor, he pulled in again.

Are you kidding me?

"Hi there, I'm sorry I forgot to introduce myself on my earlier visit. I'm Tom. Tom Lubin."

"Hi, sir. I'm Mark. Is there something I can do for you today?"

"Uh yeah, yeah. There's this, uh, rattle in my car. Any chance you can take a ride with me to figure out what it is?"

Well, at least I might get a commission out of this.

I folded myself into his two-year-old, bright orange Volvo, and we turned onto Lincoln Avenue. He chatted about the weather while I listened intently to the hum of the motor, which sounded perfect, no rattle.

"The noise usually starts up when the engine's a little warmer. I'll just drive a little farther," he said.

About two miles in, when the conversation shifted to basketball, I confirmed there was no rattle, none whatsoever. Annoyed at having wasted my time, I could not suppress the irritation in my voice when I said, "How about you just take me back to the shop, and let me out of your car?"

He did. I got out and he pulled away, an irritatingly pleasant look still on his face. *Good riddance*, I thought. *I hope that's the end of that.*

It wasn't the end, however. Nowhere near the end, in fact. Lubin showed up again a day later; this time he had a college catalog. He told me he taught chemistry at Cypress College, just a few minutes from the shop, where he also happened to be an assistant basketball coach. He wanted me to consider enrolling there so I could play ball on his team.

I rolled my eyes as I thanked him for his *extreme* interest in my life and explained I had already attended vocational school in Arizona. I had a job, and I needed to get back to work.

A couple days went by, and Lubin walked into the shop again! This time he showed up with a shoebox.

When will this guy give up?

"Open it, open it!" he exclaimed excitedly.

Basketball shoes. Size 17. *How did he know my shoe size?!*

"Thank you, Mr. Lubin, but I can't take these." I handed the shoes back, but he insisted I keep them.

I thanked him, dropped the shoes on my workbench, and got back to work on a brake job. The next week, just before we opened, I saw Tom Lubin on the other side of the door. I tried to ignore him, but he knocked persistently. The guys in the shop laughed, "Your stalker is back, Mark!" I shook my head in disbelief and stepped outside.

"Mark, good morning. I'm on my way to the gym for conditioning with the team, thought I'd see if you wanted to come join us. Getting into the gym is just as important as time on the court. If we start today, we can get you ready for—"

"Mr. Lubin, I know you mean well, but I left basketball behind three years ago. I played terribly in high school. The game never liked me, and I never liked it. I'm happy where I am. I like my job and my life. I am not interested in joining your team."

Undeterred, Lubin showed up again on Friday. He had Bruce Randall, another assistant coach at Cypress College, in tow. This time I continued to work on the car while Lubin talked at me, hoping they would get the hint. They followed me around the car like two shadows. Lubin jabbered on and on about the program at Cypress and all of the players he had helped get to the next level. Randall never uttered a word; his mouth just hung open as he gawked at me.

"The answer is still no, Mr. Lubin. I have no interest in playing for your team." Finally, after thirty minutes of doing laps around the car, they left.

The next day was Saturday, which meant no school and no Tom Lubin. *Perfect*, I thought. *I'll actually be able to get some work done.* I settled in to do a tune-up, happy to get a break from my stalker.

"Mark! Hey, I was headed to the lab today, thought I'd stop by!"

Seriously? This guy is unbelievable!

"I don't know if I explained what it is I really do.

Teaching basketball to tall guys, guys like you, is my specialty." He went on to explain he had played college ball in San Diego, and that he understood the game was different for tall men (Tom is 6'6"). He told me he had helped players like Swen Nater (who had a long career in the NBA and was ABA rookie of the year in 1974) and Rick Darnell (who played in the ABA for the Virginia Squires) go on to play professionally.

"That's great for them, and for you. I'm sorry I have never heard of those people. My customer will be back for her car in a few minutes, so good luck today."

Almost a week later on the following Friday, at the end of work, Lubin walked in with Swen Nater, a 6'11" Dutchman who played for the San Diego Clippers. Lubin acted as if Nater and I were destined to become best friends.

Of course! We are just a few inches apart in height. That obviously correlates to instantaneous friendship. Geesh!

Lubin wanted to take us both to dinner that night.

"Sorry, but I've got plans. Nice to meet you, Mr. Nater."

Incredibly, a few days later, on Tom Lubin's *fifteenth* visit, he tried a new tactic.

"Mark, let's make a deal. Give me thirty minutes on the court to show you what I know. If you don't like what you see, I promise, I'll leave you alone."

Did he just say he'd leave me alone?

"Deal."

The next day, Coach Lubin was clearly excited as he drove me to Cypress College to get those thirty minutes out of me. I brooded silently, wanting to get this over with. We

walked into the gym to discover a construction crew refin-
ishing the wood floors. Obviously not one to give up easily,
Coach Lubin led me to the courts outside. It was raining
lightly but that didn't deter him.

As I walked onto the asphalt court, a sick feeling
churned in my gut. I remembered missed shots. Awkward
attempts at rebounds. Being benched after a minute in the
game. Laughter from the crowd. *Man, I hate this game!
What am I doing here?*

But then Coach Lubin proceeded to show me things I
had never seen before. Moves designed specifically for tall
players. I had only experienced the game from the "run and
gun" perspective, a game strategy based on a fast-paced,
fast break offense. I had no idea there were aspects to this
game where I had the height, and potentially, the skill and
ability, to become an asset on the court.

Coach Lubin instructed me. "Catch the ball, take a step,
hook shot. Then try this, catch the ball, pivot, bank shot.
Always keep the ball up above your head. Don't bring it
down where the little guys can swipe it away."

It seemed too simple, and I hated to admit it, but he had
something. He told me his uncle Frank Lubin, a Lithuanian
who played on the 1932 Olympic basketball team, had
been one of the original "big men" in basketball. Frank had
taught him how to change up the game for tall players.

This was nothing like high school basketball, which had
been all about quick movements, fast breakaways, and ten-
foot jumpers. This was something I could actually do!

"Mark, your horrible high school basketball experience

wasn't your fault. Most coaches don't know what to do with big men. But being tall *is* an advantage," he said. "You can *make* it your advantage."

He had my attention. Maybe there was more to this game of basketball than I realized. By the time I learned pivot-bank shot, I decided to work with Coach Lubin. We quickly progressed from working out one or two nights a week, to working out every night. I went from mechanic to aspiring college athlete in a matter of weeks.

Eventually, my life became consumed with, and driven by, basketball. Every day at six thirty a.m., Coach Lubin picked me up at my apartment and we ran for an hour before I went to the shop. After work, I would clean the grease out of my fingernails and head back to the gym for a few more hours in the weight room. Coach Lubin yakked in my ear about basketball fundamentals the entire workout.

I struggled through sore muscles, stumbled awkwardly through agility drills, and listened to the groans from the Cypress College coaching staff as I grappled with basketball moves that were foreign to me. It was a radical time of change, and it was rough on my mind and body. As our workouts progressed, I partied less, traded in fast food for protein powder and desiccated liver, and got more sleep. After a couple of months, I gained a little more confidence, and transitioned from an out-of-shape auto mechanic to someone who resembled an athlete.

Coach Lubin was convinced from our first meeting that I had potential to be a basketball star. The rest of us were not so sure. When he began to work with me, word quickly spread of his new "project." After the Cypress coaching staff watched me play, it was obvious that I was more of an awkward uncertainty than a rising star. They were not the only ones with doubts. I was not sure I had a future in basketball either.

When it came time to commit to Cypress, I had to dig deep. It was a big risk to leave the comfort of my toolbox, and a steady paycheck, to pursue an unknown future on the court. Should I stay focused on my career in auto mechanics or push my limits and dream for more? Especially when that dream involved re-entering a sport where I had a painful history.

After much soul searching, I reached a decision. Hedging my bets, I kept my job as a mechanic. I worked in the morning, took night classes at Cypress College, and became an official member of the Cypress Charger basketball team. My fellow players embraced me and, for the first time, practice was actually enjoyable. Coach Don Johnson, the first All-American player of legendary UCLA coach John Wooden, led our team.

The day before the season opener, our starting center broke his nose in practice. Ironically, it was on my elbow (sorry, Grant Taylor)! The result was that I found myself as the starting center when the whistle blew on my first game as a college player.

The season was extraordinary: We won thirty-four games in a row, losing only two, our first and last games. I was surprised I played an integral part in my team's success. Local press began to pay attention. Television stations showed up to do stories on the mechanic-turned-junior-college-center. At the end of my freshman year, I was *stunned* to get a call from the Phoenix Suns to inform me they had chosen me in the fifth round of the NBA Draft! While I was flattered in the extreme, the offer was not guaranteed and would only translate to $30,000 a year—if I were lucky enough to make the team. That was not much more than I earned as a mechanic, so I decided to stay at Cypress College and dream bigger. That call, however, was a defining moment. It was the first time I realized that this game of basketball could be more than something I did part-time and helped further my education. It could be a career! The NBA was a distinct possibility, and I decided to get serious about this game of basketball.

My sophomore season our team won the California State Championship. There was an incredible amount of press coverage. Scouts from a number of top-tier schools from around the country—Purdue, UCLA, Washington—courted me and worked to convince me to join their team. It was surreal to be noticed and acknowledged for my basketball skills and not just my height. And frankly, the notoriety and visibility were a bit intimidating.

My life continued to change dramatically. Coach Lubin convinced me I could no longer afford to spend long hours bent over engines as it would impede my performance on the court. So he made a few phone calls and got me hired as a car salesman at a nearby Datsun dealership. (Perhaps you can picture me crammed into a tiny B210 Honeybee explaining to the customer that it is a roomy vehicle!) I picked up a second job as a bouncer at a local nightclub to help pay for books and tuition. My days started at six a.m. with a workout, followed by shooting and agility drills before classes. After school, I went to the dealership to sell cars. When the dealership closed at nine p.m., I headed to my job as a bouncer at Hofs Hut Disco. I stood next to a cigarette machine and checked IDs until two a.m. I worked long, hard hours off the court, and even harder on the court.

In those two years at Cypress College Tom Lubin taught me a new way to play basketball and a new way to think. He emphasized the importance of a strong belief in myself, the value of being a team player, and the power of hard work. He helped me overcome the deep-seated fears and insecurities I had carried from my time as a benchwarmer in high school.

From Coach Don Johnson I learned about execution, and evolved into what he called a TSU player: tough, smart, and unselfish. The goal for every member of our team was to be a TSU player, to execute our role to the best of our ability, and to work together. The experiences I had and lessons learned during those two years have continued to assist me in every step of my life journey.

One critical component to the lessons I learned along the way is that personal preparation is essential to both individual and team success. As I mentioned, at the end of the basketball season at Cypress Junior College schools from around the country recruited me. Ultimately, the lure of UCLA and Coach Larry Brown proved too strong to resist. UCLA was a premier basketball program at the time.

Coach Johnson and Swen Nater, both of whom were UCLA alumni, also influenced my decision. I was excited to play for the NCAA dynasty I had watched as a child. I also knew that as a UCLA Bruin I would have the visibility necessary to propel me to the NBA.

The year before I signed with the team, UCLA was the runner-up in the NCAA National Championship game, so expectations for the team were sky high the year I signed on. The stars seemed aligned for me since a number of big men had graduated the previous year and my chances for time on the court were greatly improved.

It wasn't long, however, before I realized things would not play out as I anticipated. Once again, I found myself sitting on the end of the bench, playing only a few minutes each game. I was discouraged and didn't know what to do. So I did what I always did in situations like that, I called my trusted coach and friend, Tom Lubin.

I expressed my frustration to him and conveyed my fears that another stint as a benchwarmer would wholly derail my NBA dreams.

"Then work harder," he replied, ever the pragmatist. "If you're not playing in the games, make the practices your games. Be the first guy at practice and the last one to leave."

So that's exactly what I did.

At first I set small goals. Every ten-minute scrimmage I told myself, "Okay, Mark, get three offensive rebounds, two blocked shots, and two dunks." I knew if I had any chance of a future in basketball, I couldn't waste any opportunity to get better, even if I went unnoticed at the time.

It's a similar situation on the basketball court as it is in the office. You can't always control who your boss is or your work environment, but you can control your approach to personal preparation, teamwork, and dedication to your job. Coach Lubin helped me do just that as I struggled at UCLA. I prepared myself to be successful, so when my day came to play, I was ready. Was it always fun? No. Was it miserable many days? Yes. However, I was determined to get better. There was always something I could do to improve my game. I ached for the opportunity to help my team win. I resolved to work hard until that chance arrived, and I could be an asset when I was called upon.

During my career at UCLA, my time on the court did not increase. In fact, it actually *decreased*. I became more and more frustrated and relied heavily on Coach Lubin for emotional support.

I talked to him every few days and he never ceased to encourage me. He would say, "This is a short period of time, Mark. The big picture is still down the road." He regularly drove up from Orange County, and we met at Tito's Tacos or Johnnie's Pastrami in West LA to talk. He helped me stay focused and keep my eye on the prize: a place on an NBA team.

After my first year at UCLA, Coach Larry Brown took a job in the NBA with the New Jersey Nets. UCLA hired Larry Farmer, who had played under legendary Coach John Wooden in the early '70s. *Whew*, I thought, *I finally have a chance!*

Soon after he arrived, I went into Coach Farmer's office

and said, "Sir, I really want to play next year. What can I work on this summer to ensure I am prepared to play next season?" He thought a bit, wrote down ten things, and handed me his list. The list included things like improve jump shot, foot speed, and low post play, and work on strength and conditioning.

Encouraged, I practiced those ten things diligently that summer. I returned in the fall much better prepared. Coach Farmer even pulled me aside and told me how impressed he was with my improvement.

Grateful to be noticed, I felt confident, ready to contribute and do whatever was required of me.

Unfortunately, Coach Farmer had different plans, in the form of a new freshman center with big potential. So there I was, stuck at the end of the bench again.

Let's just say that my senior year at UCLA was long and filled with disappointment. I saw the court less than I had my junior year, but I decided to focus on what I could control and work hard. I worked on my own, with Coach Lubin, and at practice.

Every day, until the last day of the season, I was the first to arrive at practice and the last to leave. When Coach Farmer left me off the roster on our final road trip to Oregon; after I threw the trash can lid across Pauley Pavilion; after I went back to my apartment and felt sorry for myself; I did what I always did—I called Coach Lubin.

His response was not what I expected.

"Oh, that's great Mark, we can work out then! Grab your shoes, get in the car, and drive down here." I wanted to be with my team, or on a beach—anywhere but in a basketball gym. Coach Lubin, as usual, persisted, and convinced me to drive to Orange County.

As my team closed out the season in battles with Oregon and Oregon State, I was in the Cypress College gym with Coach Lubin. We worked on my game, improved my skill set, and prepared for a future opportunity.

It was a devastating low point for me. I was thoroughly discouraged by the abrupt and dissatisfying end to my college career. Once again, my future in basketball felt bleak. But I would not give up. I kept working. I just was not sure where my efforts would lead.

Ever the optimist, Coach Lubin took me to San Diego to watch Swen Nater play with the San Diego Clippers. After the game, we sat down with head coach Paul Silas and assistant coaches Pete Babcock and Bill Westphal and asked for advice. They suggested I attend a try-out camp in New Jersey that attracted a couple of NBA scouts. So I scraped together enough money for a flight and hotel and flew to New Jersey.

It was an experience I will never forget.

On the flight, I sat next to a nice young woman who offered to have her parents give me a ride to my motel in Jersey City. I had a paper with the addresses of three motels, all of which were close to the site of our games. The young woman's family dropped me off at the first motel on the list. The first thing I noticed, aside from the bars that covered the check-in window, was the adjacent sign with room rates listed by the hour! I cautiously walked up to the window and explained I was there for a basketball camp. I held the paper up against the glass for the man to read. He looked at my attire, read through the list, grimaced, and said, "Son, this is the best one out of the three." I checked in and unpacked my bag in the seedy motel room that would become my home for the next three days. I worked hard and concentrated on my execution. I put everything I had into my time on the court, and hoped it would provide an opportunity to reach the next level. The camp went well and Al Menendez, a scout for the New Jersey Nets, noticed me. He also happened to be a friend of Utah Jazz coach Frank Layden, and told Layden about me.

Later that year I was drafted by the struggling Utah franchise, and a coach who knew he could use a strong defensive player—or at least someone taller than every other guy on the court!

I finally began to see the result of my preparation, the fruit of so many long days and nights spent in training.

When I look back on the years that led to my first moment on The Salt Palace floor, outfitted in a Utah Jazz jersey, I am grateful for every second I spent in preparation.

That time equipped me to play against the biggest names in NBA history—from Larry Bird, Dr. J, and Michael Jordan, to Magic Johnson, Charles Barkley, and Shaquille O'Neal.

There were definitely days that summer of '78 I hated to hear the honk of Coach Lubin's horn at six thirty in the morning. Yes, I grumbled when he badgered me through another agility regimen at ten at night. I gritted my teeth through endless scrimmages at UCLA with the fruitless hope the coach would reward me with a few more minutes of game-time.

Every exhaustive work out, every extra hour at the gym, every time I dared to believe in myself despite the setbacks, all prepared me for the day my opportunity would arrive. And it did finally arrive when Coach Frank Layden of the Utah Jazz called me on June 29, 1982. That was the day my NBA future began, the one Coach Lubin had inspired me to dream of when he pulled into my tire shop.

The lessons learned, the physical and mental growth, the work, didn't end when I became an NBA player. It is ongoing. I continue to apply those commitments today as a team building expert, speaker, author, and entrepreneur.

What are your possibilities? What are your capabilities? What can you do now to develop yourself into a better contributor? Make self-improvement an everyday part of your professional and personal life. Be open. Use expert sources, mentors, and trainers, and learn everything you can. Ask others what you can do to get better. Set goals and put them in motion. And remember to work! As a kid who struggled on the high school court, I can attest there is no substitute for good old-fashioned tenacity to becoming a real game changer.

With the Four Commitments, you will have what it takes to get in the game and stay there, no matter where you are today. You will learn how to consistently play at the top of your game, and *win at anything*. As you turn these pages, I will become your coach. I will help you discover what others have shown me: the four secrets that will utterly transform your career, organization, and life. As you put these commitments into play, you will realize your potential, and the limitless possibilities you and your team have together.

COMMITMENT #1

KNOW YOUR JOB

CHAPTER 3

"I've missed more than 9,000 shots in my career. I've lost almost 300 games. Twenty-six times I've been trusted to take the game winning shot and missed. I've failed over and over and over again in my life. And that is why I succeed."

– MICHAEL JORDAN

I WAS NO STRANGER to summer pick-up ball in Los Angeles. While at Cypress Junior College, Coach Lubin had me play games at Compton College, Crenshaw High School, and other inner-city venues. He said, "If you want to get better, you have to play against the best players." The players didn't get better than those in downtown LA.

I showed up in every gym and played in every game possible. Smaller, faster, better players surrounded me, but I was as determined and committed as they were. A few seasoned players felt I was woefully unprepared and inexperienced for the level of skill and competitiveness required in these leagues. Perhaps they were right, but they underestimated my resolve.

One of the leagues I played in regularly was Joe Weakley's Run, Shoot, and Dunk League. Those games got very physical, and I quickly learned to hold my own in the paint. One game in particular, I had several blocks on a small guard from the opposing team. After the fourth consecutive rejection, he got so frustrated that he ran straight at me, jumped up, and planted two feet in my chest in an attempt to take me out. His attempt was unsuccessful, and I chased him out of the gym. My teammate Darwin Cook, who later played several seasons in the NBA for the New Jersey Nets, told me it was in that moment that he knew I would be okay in the league.

As it turned out, the best place to compete and perform was in the pick-up games at UCLA. Those games were unparalleled. Not just anyone was allowed to play. You had to prove your worth on the court.

The summer between my junior and senior year at eight a.m. every day I was at the old Men's Gym. I worked out and played in pick-up games in the third floor gym. It was outdated and malodorous. It was also familiar and comfortable, my home away from home.

Every afternoon, however, that gym transformed into something radically different. It was filled with players like Magic Johnson, James Worthy, Michael Cooper, and Kiki Vandeweghe. The line-ups read like an NBA All-Star roster.

There was a list taped to the wall and when you got there, you put your name on. Games were played to seven points. The team that won stayed on the court and played the next five players on the list. It went on like that all afternoon.

The structure and pace of the summer games was much different from traditional games. They were fast and intense. Quick, agile guards would sprint from one end of the court to the other. For a big man like me, it was difficult to keep up. But as Coach Lubin had foreseen, as I competed against a higher caliber of talent, the level of my performance increased.

One day I found myself chasing a guard named Rocket Rod Foster as he ran up and down the court. He was simply the fastest human being I have ever seen. He would get to the basket about the time I crossed half court. I couldn't figure out what to do. I was out on the court, but I was not in the game.

Frustrated, I decided to take a break on the sidelines. I bent over huffing and puffing, trying to catch my breath and regain my composure. *I don't know, maybe I just can't compete at this level. Maybe I don't have what it takes.*

At that precise moment, a large hand clamped down on my shoulder. I turned around and stood face to face with 7'2" Wilt Chamberlain, arguably the greatest basketball player of all time. Wilt had retired from the NBA a few years earlier but came to the gym every day to workout with the young guys. He grabbed my shoulder, spun me around, looked me straight in the eye, pointed to Rocket Rod Foster, and said, "First of all, young fella, you are never going to catch that man!"

"Thanks, Wilt. I already figured that out."

"More importantly," he said, "*it's not your job.* Come with me." Wilt grasped me by the arm, took me out on the court, and positioned me right in front of the basket. "Let me tell you what your job is. You see this basket? Your job is to stop players from getting there. Your job is to make them miss their shot, collect the rebound, throw it up to the guard, let them go down to the other end and score. Then your job is to cruise up to half court and see what is going on."

I smiled as Wilt continued, "I've been watching you play. I've seen the skill you have at defense. This is where you need to focus. This is your job."

A light bulb went on, and my life on the court was forever changed. It was the "aha" that shifted my perspective, and the flash of clarity that launched my career.

Wilt showed me what my job was, and how concentrating on that job and performing it well would benefit my team. It became clear what I needed to focus on and what I needed to let go. I wasn't that fast, or that great at scoring, but I did have a talent for defense and preventing others from scoring goals. Wilt Chamberlain recognized and defined that talent for me. That five-minute conversation changed how I saw my contribution to my team. Within five years of that conversation, I broke the NBA record for most blocked shots in a single season: 456. It is still the record today.

Because I was receptive to Wilt's advice, I understood and embraced my job. I stopped trying to do *everything* and focused on *mastering one thing*—defending the basket. He helped me realize that trying to "do it all" does not lead to success.

A perfect example of this occurred in the 2015 NBA Finals. It was a showdown between two of the best teams in the NBA, the Golden State Warriors and the Cleveland Cavaliers.

LeBron James, one of the greatest basketball players in the world, led the Cleveland Cavaliers. He had All-Stars Kyrie Irving and Kevin Love by his side, and many people believed they were the favorite to win the championship. Then Kevin Love went down with an injury early in the playoffs, and Irving was hurt in the first game of the Finals. With both of them out for the series, and no comparable replacements, LeBron James had to manage on his own.

The Golden State Warriors featured the talented Steph Curry, Klay Thompson, and Draymond Green, but their greatest strength was in the way they played *team* basketball.

LeBron battled valiantly, literally trying to do everything himself. Because of his incredible skill and competitiveness, he was able to propel the Cavaliers to a 2–1 series lead after three games. As the series wore on, James grew weary. The Warriors, however, continued to share the ball and work as a team. They took control of the series and won the last three games. Ultimately, they won the championship.

Even the greatest player in the world cannot do it by himself.

Too often, we believe we alone have to possess every skill our market requires. As a dentist, you think you need to be an expert in dental care, but also patient acquisition, finance, and facility management. As an owner of a retail franchise, you may feel you have to be an expert at merchandise placement, inventory management, and human resources.

The reality is you may be good at several things, but you cannot be an expert in everything. Let go of that false expectation for yourself. If you're in management, let go of that expectation for your employees, too. You do not want to be the coach who sits a valuable player on the bench just because he doesn't meet your expectations in every way.

I think back with gratitude on the wise coaches I have had, like Tom Lubin and Frank Layden, who allowed me to make mistakes. They were patient and helped me grow into someone whose achievements benefited the entire team. More importantly, they taught me to focus on what I did well, not on what I didn't.

I asked Coach Lubin why he never gave up on me and he said, "I'd had some success with Swen Nater and Rick Darnell—neither of those guys played in high school but they were big; 6'11" and 6'10". You were even taller. I saw your potential. I thought, 'What the heck? We just won the state championship and here's a very tall guy within a half a mile of the college. He may be the best of them all.'"

When I reminded him how raw I was and how little I knew about basketball, Coach Lubin said, "Most people, when they see someone as tall as you, Mark, they assume the guy can just do this stuff. But I knew it would be a step-by-step process. I was patient because I had worked with people in the past who also started from zero. You were patient with yourself, too. You got there because you and I dared to dream, to work hard in the off seasons, and to prepare you to have a long career."

Great perspective, right? It was this viewpoint that

got me to the NBA. I clearly remember the moment my work paid off, when I discovered that others noticed I had something special to contribute to our team. It was early December my rookie season with the Jazz and we were on the road to face the Dallas Mavericks, which was an NBA expansion team at that time. Coach Layden put me in the game late in the second quarter. In my first few minutes of play, I blocked six shots! After I swiped the ball away from the glass the sixth time, I happened to glance over at the Jazz bench as I ran to the other end of the court. I watched Coach Layden whip around wide-eyed and look at his assistants, Phil Johnson and Scott Layden. The three of them smiled and nodded at each other. It was the first time I felt sure I could compete in the league and be a valuable asset to my team. I kept my focus on defense and blocking shots and left the scoring to my teammates Adrian Dantley and Darrell Griffith.

Honor your role and allow others to honor theirs.

Once I shifted my focus, and concentrated on my job, magic happened. That was when I realized I *am* a basketball player and traded my life as an auto mechanic for my dream to become an NBA player.

That is the power of knowing your job.

CHAPTER 4

"I'll do whatever it takes to win games, whether it's sitting on a bench waving a towel, handing a cup of water to a teammate, or hitting the game-winning shot."

— KOBE BRYANT

M Y THIRD YEAR in the NBA the Utah Jazz were on a roll. We had a string of successes for the first time in team history and had finally become popular in Salt Lake City. Season ticket sales were up and fans came out to support us. However, since winning was new for our franchise, our fans' backing always felt tenuous.

Midway through the season we had a string of losses. After the third loss in a row, the fans called for everyone's head, including mine. They held up signs in the arena that said, "Fire Frank!" "Trade Mark!" and the media jumped on the bandwagon. It was hard not to listen to the barrage of outside noise, and it was disheartening, to say the least.

After another loss at home, I grabbed our assistant coach, Phil Johnson, and asked him for advice. Johnson was the former head coach for the Sacramento Kings and was known for his strength in strategy and game plan development. He was also levelheaded and always kept things in perspective. He suggested we go out after the game and talk.

"How do I deal with this criticism?" I asked. Johnson didn't hesitate. "Mark, what you do for our team doesn't always show up on the stat sheet. You help us win games. Period. People who don't understand basketball don't get that. Don't listen to them. Here's what I want you to do. Cancel your subscription to the newspaper. Don't listen to the radio. And don't pay attention to the TV. Those are distractions you don't need."

Anxious for a reprieve from the outside chatter, I immediately took his advice.

That conversation changed *everything* for me. I knew Johnson supported me unconditionally and with his support, I was able to relax and block out the negative noise. I made my job—blocking shots and being a great defender for my team—my single focus.

Let go of stress and stop worrying, especially over things that are not your responsibility. I had allowed myself to carry the weight of every jeer from the stands and every negative comment from sports reporters, even when the criticism was not aimed at me directly. If I had let that continue, the strain would have paralyzed me and I would not have performed well on the court. When I rid myself of the idea that I was solely responsible for the success and future of the franchise, I was able to focus on my job.

Coach Johnson showed me it was the coach's job to manage the team, the owner's job to manage the future of the franchise, and my job to block shots and snag rebounds. As each member of our team did their job, the big picture came back into focus and we began to win again.

On a fishing trip with my friend Richard Smith, who was formerly the International Sales Manager for Eli Lily, he shared a great example of how knowing your job and playing to your strengths helps everyone win. Rich took over a sales territory in Eastern Europe that was fraught with poor morale and declining sales. The sales team consisted of a group of physicians from China, Poland, Germany, and Russia. The diversity of languages, cultures, and backgrounds created communication barriers and made getting to know one another difficult. To combat these challenges, Smith planned team building trips so the group could spend time getting to know one another away from work. On one of these trips, each physician took a personality test, which pinpointed their strengths. The teams were then reorganized to ensure that each member was in a position that played to those strengths. The results were staggering. In just a few years, sales went from six million dollars to hundreds of millions of dollars!

Sterling Nielsen, president and CEO of Mountain America Credit Union, believes it is vital to help employees understand their role in the organization. I have spoken to MACU's work groups many times, and I am always impressed with the results of his applied philosophy. As the head of a financial institution that spans Utah, Idaho, Arizona, New Mexico, and Nevada, he said, "I like to surround myself with people who are smarter than me, who have skills that complement my weaknesses. I know where my weaknesses are, and I make sure I have people who are strong in those areas. It's important for the organization to have that balance. That's how I've put together the management team in order to make sure our organization is as successful as it can be."

When you focus on doing your job and letting others do theirs, you and the organization succeed. I was fortunate to play with the greatest point guard in NBA history, John Stockton. Stockton was inducted into the Naismith Basketball Hall of Fame in 2009, and holds the record for most assists (15,806) and steals (32,065) in an NBA career. The point guard on a basketball team is like the quarterback on a football team. He has to know the play, understand what each player is supposed to do, and anticipate everyone's position at any given time. He can then distribute the ball so the team can score. Top-notch guards like Stockton play to each player's strengths. Stockton knew exactly how each of us liked to receive the pass to ensure success. We did it thousands of times throughout the season. We could do it in our sleep.

John Stockton was the consummate teammate. Like most great players, Stockton was ultra-competitive. Every time he stepped on the court, he accepted nothing less than a win. He was not concerned with personal stats or praise, he only wanted to make our team better and beat the competition. That kind of collaboration and teamwork is essential to success.

WHAT HAPPENS WHEN the synergy on a team is disrupted? Jack Pelo, president and CEO of Swire Coca-Cola, USA has had a lot of experience with change and disruption. As one of Coca-Cola's largest US bottling and distribution partners, Swire Coca-Cola has grown rapidly since acquiring several smaller bottlers throughout the western US. As I prepared to speak to Pelo's team at their annual sales meeting, Jack shared how unsettling change can be for employees. They feel nervous, unsure of their job security, and uncertain what the new company will expect of them. He said he has learned it is important to tell the team exactly what their roles will be, and also to show them. For example, when Swire Coca-Cola acquired a facility in Denver, Colorado, Swire sent a group of managers to work alongside the Denver team, to share Swire's management style and operating practices. Pelo said, "It takes some time to actually sit down with people, talk through it, and then work beside them. But it's worthwhile because that's how people learn. I feel strongly about that."

Although the adjustment was not without its initial hurdles, this hands-on approach eased what could have been a difficult transition.

When a team has synergy, it delivers consistency and excellence, which is critical for any organization's success. In sports, consistency is both desired and expected. If I blocked ten shots, Stockton had thirteen assists, and Malone put up 30 plus points in a game, the home crowd expected the same double-digit performance the next game.

In my post-basketball life, I am co-owner of two fine dining restaurants in Salt Lake City, Tuscany and Franck's. In the restaurant industry, you're only as good as the last meal you've served. I've seen firsthand that for diners, like athletes, it is all about consistency. From the hosts at the front door, to the line cooks, servers, and head chef, the performance of our entire team working in concert is critical to creating an extraordinary dining experience. That attention to detail and synergy is why we have been fortunate to receive top Zagat ratings year after year.

Hiring well is also vital to consistency. Take the role of a chef, for instance. People assume a chef has to be an elite and amazing culinary artist. While they certainly need excellent culinary skills, the greatest asset a chef can bring to the table is kitchen management. A chef who truly knows their job understands how to manage labor, maximize ordering, and attract—and keep—talented support staff.

Over the years, I have seen great chefs who came in with stellar reputations, but they didn't last long because they were poor kitchen managers, and didn't get along with other members of the team. They didn't grasp how to lead or encourage others to bring their collective strengths together. They alienated themselves right out of a job, despite their superb culinary skills.

Success in Commitment #1, *Know Your Job*, comes when you understand what you can and cannot do, stick to your job, focus on the big picture, and maintain a cohesive synergy. As you put Commitment #1 into action, you and your team will create a solid foundation for success.

CHAPTER 5

"Do not permit what you cannot do to interfere with what you can do."

- JOHN WOODEN

A S SOON AS I IMPLEMENTED Wilt Chamberlain's advice on the court, the trajectory of my basketball career changed course. I had a goal. I had a purpose. I had something concrete to focus on. I understood that I needed to execute my role to help my team win basketball games.

From that point forward, my goal was to become the best defensive player possible. I spent most of my time working on footwork, blocking shots, and rebounding. I no longer worried about how many points I scored or attempted to keep up with the quicker, more athletic players.

What Chamberlain taught me revolutionized my game and built on the "big man" foundation Coach Lubin laid out for me. I doubted Coach Lubin when he showed up at the tire shop claiming he could show me how to play the game differently. I thought I knew all there was to know about how to play basketball, but he challenged my assumptions. When I took a closer look at strategies I had never considered or had overlooked, a new world opened up to me.

In that same vein, there have been times I've introduced Commitment #1, *Know Your Job,* to a leadership team and have seen a doubtful look on their faces. I'm sure it is the same look I gave Coach Lubin when he said he could teach me something new. Many leaders wonder if "knowing your job" is too simple a concept to be transformative. Once they consider a different perspective and accept that success in Commitment #1 rests with them defining each role in their organization, including their own, things start to change and improve.

I spoke to a team of consultants who provide marketing support for companies, from small start-ups to Fortune 500 corporations. They work with CEOs, internal marketing, communications, and product development departments, as well as front-line employees. The companies cover a wide array of industries—aviation, financial services, jewelry, and cosmetics, among others. From their unique vantage point outside the organization, they can see what effectively contributes to a company's growth and success, and what trips them up. They reported the biggest obstacle to success they encounter, in companies of every size, is the lack of clearly defined roles for employees.

They gave the example of a client who started their business with a handful of executives and staff at the company headquarters, and a few dozen sales representatives scattered across the country. In less than five years, the company had grown dramatically and employed tens of thousands of sales reps, who worked with hundreds of thousands of customers across the US and Canada.

Their growth was so explosive that the head office had to continually scramble to keep up with everything from product development to marketing and fulfillment. They hired and hired. Before they knew it, they were housed in a building filled with more than 500 people. While all of the corporate staff were well-qualified individuals, the company found productivity did not increase, and employee satisfaction actually declined.

It was apparent to the consultants that although individual job duties had been outlined on paper, and people had a general sense of their responsibilities, nobody knew where their job ended and their colleague's began. It wasn't uncommon in team meetings for two or three employees to discover that they, unknown to the others, had been tasked to work on the same project.

Employees were confused and frustrated by the constant overlap and unclear division of responsibilities. Some got caught up in internal competition while others became passive, thinking, "Why try? Someone else will do my job anyway."

When new management finally stepped in, one of the first things they tackled was defining clear roles for every person in every position, from management to front-line employees. Within a year, the company was a united force with direction and focus, and reaped success in every aspect of the business.

It's not enough to draw up general job descriptions for new employees to read through once, and then send them on their way. It is critical to be specific when you're defining employee roles. You must take the time to decide who will do what, then lay out how individual responsibilities align with the roles of others on the team. Once this is in place, it's important to monitor how things are going, and evaluate the results over time. Sometimes the initial assignments may not work and adjustments have to be made.

I personally discovered how crucial it is that every facet of every role you hold be defined by your leaders. Early in my career, I was assigned by my teammates to be the team player representative to the NBPA (National Basketball Players Association), the Union that represents players in the NBA. My job was to be a conduit of information from the Union leadership in New York to my teammates and address any Collective Bargaining Agreement (CBA) issues with team management, which could range from how many appearances the team required to how much meal money we received while on the road. (The CBA is the operating agreement that defines the working relationship between the Players and the NBA.) It was not a popular position. It also entailed discussing all workplace grievances with the team owner, coaches, and management. No one wanted this job, which is the reason I, as a young, inexperienced team member, ended up with the assignment. However, I never received a job description and I had no idea what the role entailed or what was expected of me. Frankly, I did not give the role much thought or attention as it seemed so disconnected from my job on the court.

Shortly after I took the assignment, we were in San Antonio for a game. We had to travel to Houston the following day for another game. In this financially strapped era of the NBA, many team owners tried to save money by hiring buses for travel or putting players in coach seats on flights. Coach Layden had scheduled a bus for our team to make the trip to Houston from San Antonio, and some of the veteran players were irritated we would not be on a plane. I happened to have a conference call that day with the NBPA team representatives and union director Larry Fleisher. The players on my team who were unhappy with our planned bus trip encouraged me to ask Fleisher why we had to take a bus instead of a plane as the CBA required.

At the end of the call, Fleisher asked if there were any issues that needed to be addressed. I dutifully brought up the question of the bus ride to Houston, as my teammates had requested. I was put on hold and asked to wait. Unbeknownst to me, while I was on hold, phone calls were exchanged between Larry Fleisher and the NBA commissioner, and the NBA commissioner and Coach Layden. I had stirred up a hornet's nest of epic proportion. I had unwittingly violated my coach's trust, involved the league in a minor team travel matter, and brought unwanted scrutiny and focus to our team. Needless to say, when I got off that phone call, Coach Layden hunted me down. He was beyond furious! (Have you ever seen a seven-footer try to crawl under a bus seat?)

As it turned out, Layden had thoughtfully pre-arranged the bus because it was quicker and more convenient than any of the available flights. It was also more comfortable and less stressful for the players, as it was stocked with sandwiches, drinks, snacks, and TVs (unheard of at the time, and not available on planes). My teammates and I were unaware of any of this. I had only listened to the concerns of the veteran players and never considered a conversation with our Coach regarding our travel arrangements. I had not done my job. Had I taken the time to apply Commitment #1, and really known what my job as player representative entailed, this situation would never have happened. I would have taken in all sides of the issue before taking anything to the league. From that experience, I quickly learned everything I could about my job as team player representative and gave those duties the attention they deserved. I grew as a player and a person and my role on our team became more valuable and impactful.

The more careful and precise you are in defining roles, the more likely you will produce the results you want: higher productivity, employee retention, better customer satisfaction, and increased sales. On the other hand, if employees' or team members' roles are ambiguous, you invite inefficiency, a dissatisfied workforce, unhappy customers, and lackluster sales.

Once management defines roles for each team member and position, it is vital to communicate the nuances of those roles often and in multiple ways. You cannot train an employee one time and assume he or she will internalize everything they need to know. Just as an NBA team practices hours every day and coaches continually watch film of opponents then make adjustments in individual roles for the upcoming game, successful employee teams require frequent reinforcement, support, and guidance to understand and fulfill expectations. Eighteenth-century author Samuel Johnson said it well: "People need to be reminded more often than they need to be instructed."

REPETITION IS ANOTHER KEY to success in mastering your job. A coach who believed strongly in the importance of repeating excellence was John Wooden. Coach Wooden was one of the greatest and most revered college basketball coaches of all time. He coached the UCLA Bruins to ten national championships in a twelve-year period and won an unprecedented seven championships in a row. He was renowned for the way he taught, coached, and inspired. Coaches, business managers, and leaders alike often quote John Wooden.

One of my favorite quotes from him is, "The importance of repetition until automaticity cannot be overstated. Repetition is the key to learning." Whether in basketball or your field of work, nothing beats doing a task over and over until you become an expert in it.

IT IS ALSO IMPORTANT for every team member to realize mistakes *will* be made. No one is perfect, and errors and miscommunication are more likely to happen when new positions are created or new employees are hired. If you let your team know that you expect there will be some rough spots, they will feel safe to learn and push through mistakes.

In my early days with the Jazz, Coach Layden transitioned our team away from the up-tempo style of play, used when prolific scorer Pistol Pete Maravich had been with the team, toward a more methodical approach, based on defense and running on opportunity. This was fortunate for me as it fit perfectly into my style of play, but I was not a seasoned player and I had a lot to learn.

When I arrived in Utah, Coach Layden let me know what he expected of me and defined my role with the team. Then he let me get to work. In my effort to figure things out, there were many balls dropped out of bounds. I was hard on myself, which only made things worse. When you get frustrated, you play frustrated, and it can become a downward spiral. Frank would yell at me from the sidelines, "You already made one mistake; don't compound it with another one! Get your ass back to the other end of the floor and play defense!"

I did, and eventually the awkward kid from Westminster High School transformed into a two-time NBA Defensive Player of the Year.

With a priority on communication, and a tolerance for mistakes, everyone thrives. Frequent communication and support helps people strengthen their skills, eliminate errors, and fill their defined roles more efficiently.

Sometimes, those roles are unexpected, or not what people anticipate. On the Jazz, the teammates who stood out to me were not always the ones who scored the most points or received major headlines. Two of the best teammates I had were Thurl Bailey and Ty Corbin.

Bailey was the seventh overall draft pick out of North Carolina State, where his team won a national championship. Corbin played college basketball at DePaul before being drafted and was an adept scorer and great all-around player. Both of them were renowned for their ability to score.

However, our team already had Karl Malone. The offense ran through Malone, and he took the majority of shots. Malone is, without question, one of the greatest scorers to play in the NBA. He averaged 25 points per game in his career and is the second-most prolific scorer in NBA history, second only to Kareem Abdul-Jabbar. With statistics like that, it was imperative to get the ball to Malone.

Though they were excellent shooters, Bailey and Corbin were asked to take a different, more supportive role for the sake of our team.

I asked Bailey for his take on his experience. How did he adjust from college superstar, under legendary Coach Jimmy Valvano, to a valued utility player with the Jazz? He admitted it was tough. However, he made a conscious decision to accept his new position, and to master his job. He said, "My mentality was that I would make the sacrifice. The coach came to me with his plan and I wanted to be a part of that success story. Even if my ego didn't quite agree, I would do what he asked."

He said he had an advantage by watching from the bench. It allowed him to observe the game, see where the other team's weaknesses were, and identify what we as a team needed to do to win. "When I went in for a substitution, I already had an idea what Larry Bird was going to do, and I wasn't going to make it easy for him. I learned that it wasn't just about starting a game—I was in there with the team when it mattered most, at crunch time."

Bailey found the upside to his new role and learned how it fit in the big picture. His attitude is reminiscent of the one taken by the players on the second team at UCLA who sat on the bench with me. Rather than complain, we made a pact. We decided to do everything we could to beat the first team in daily practice. Our goal was to make the first team better, to challenge and push the starters. It helped both the first and second team to improve, and it gave us a sense of purpose coming off the bench.

Unfortunately, unlike Bailey and Corbin, not everyone chooses to embrace his role.

Over the years, I have seen players who want to be "the man," and refuse to accept anything less than a starring role, regardless of what position the team needs filled. Players with this scarcity mentality believe that if they give up something for the good of the team, it will cost them personally. When a player bounces from one team to the next, regardless of their talent, chances are high that player refused to adjust to a team system. I understand that when you have skills you want to show them off. However, it takes more than a group of talented, skilled individuals to create a winning team. It also requires players who understand that not all roles are starring ones and embrace the ones they have fully.

When you focus on what you do well, you empower yourself to excel and give others the space and freedom to excel at their jobs. When everyone focuses on what he or she does best, you create a solid foundation of camaraderie and teamwork.

When people do not understand their role, they tend to compare themselves to others when what is really required to get to the next level of mastery is honest self-assessment. Take stock of your own talents and skills, and determine how you can better leverage them.

PEOPLE OFTEN TALK ABOUT John Stockton's endless assists as being selfless, but he begs to differ. "People have told me I was unselfish my whole career because I passed the ball," says Stockton frankly. "I think I may have been the most selfish guy on the team when it all comes down to it, because I really wanted to win."

Stockton was *that* competitive. It often felt as if he could command our plays by mere thought alone, like, *By God I'm going to give you the ball and you're going to score and we're going to win, so you'd better get in position because it's coming!* His drive to win—as part of a team, not individually—guided his actions. He instinctively understood Commitment #1. By doing his job, he knew the team stood a better chance of winning.

Commitment #1, **Know Your Job**, is powerful and transformative. It elevated me from a collegiate benchwarmer to an NBA player. My determination and repeated effort to embrace and execute my role led me from relative obscurity at the beginning of my rookie season to a starting center in a matter of a few short months.

A fourth-round selection in the NBA draft, as the 72nd

overall pick, is not a typical entry in the league for NBA All-Stars. In fact, only a handful of players selected after the *second* round have gone on to become All-Stars. *No* other fourth-round NBA pick has become a starter after just fifty games. I am the only one.

When you know your job, embrace your role, and work to excel at it, you will lead your team to greater heights.

QUESTIONS & EXERCISES

On a piece of paper or on your computer, write down the answers to the following questions. I've provided lists for both common character traits and skills, but don't be limited by them if you don't see a trait or skill that applies to you.

- What do you feel is your most valuable character trait? (See list on the following page for examples.)

- On a scale from 1 to 10, how well are you currently leveraging that trait?

- How could you leverage that trait more?

- What do you feel is your greatest skill? (See list on the following page for examples.)

- On a scale from 1 to 10, how well are you currently leveraging that skill?

- How could you leverage that skill more?

- Ask three people what they see as your greatest character trait and skill. How do you see yourself, and how do others see you? What can you learn from your results?

Character Traits:

- Enthusiasm
- Honesty
- Creativity
- Fairness
- Kindness
- Integrity
- Clarity
- Confidence
- Loyalty
- Determination

Skills:

- Planning
- Organizing
- Strategizing
- Coaching
- Leading
- Instructing
- Troubleshooting
- Motivating
- Creating
- Analyzing

COMMITMENT #2

DO WHAT YOU'RE ASKED TO DO

CHAPTER 6

"My best skill was that I was coachable. I was a sponge and aggressive to learn."

– MICHAEL JORDAN

WHEN I JOINED THE JAZZ, I had less basketball experience than most NBA players, but I had tenacity and determination in spades. I was focused and ready to concentrate on my defensive prowess. So I was very surprised when Coach Layden told me he wanted to get me started on dribbling drills. "Coach, I'm not allowed to dribble the ball," I explained.

He was taken aback. "What do you mean, you're not allowed to dribble the ball?"

"I mean just that. I am not allowed to dribble the ball. I *never* dribble the ball."

Coach Layden was stunned, and he quickly dismissed the input I'd received from previous coaches as ridiculous. He gave me a series of ball-handling drills to practice every day. "You are uncomfortable with the ball in your hands, and I want to change that," he said. "It's not that I want you to dribble in the games, but if you grab a rebound and need to dribble out of traffic, I want you to be comfortable with that."

He started me on a series of drills to improve my dexterity. I passed the ball from one hand to the other, then around my knees, then around my head. I did figure eights between my knees with the ball. Then I moved on to dribbling drills. I dribbled between my legs, between my legs in figure eights, left hand dribbles, right hand dribbles, dribbling with two balls. I dribbled one ball in a static position with my left hand and simultaneously dribbled around my right leg with my right hand. Then I did the opposite. I did full court dribbles, then full court dribbles with two balls. I worked on crossover dribbles, behind the back dribbles, and spin dribbles—all to improve my competency with the basketball. As Coach Layden predicted and planned, over time I felt more comfortable when I handled the ball. This was no small feat. Big men don't usually spend much time with the ball, and I spent less time than most. My job was to get rebounds and get the ball out to my teammates. It wasn't that I had never worked on ball handling before; I had worked on it with the rest of the team in practice. But Coach Layden looked at that skill from a different perspective. He wanted me to be ready when the competition got tough. He had me do those exercises because it would help my confidence on the court. And it did. My confidence improved and so did the team's trust in me.

Commitment #2 is **Do What You're Asked to Do**. Your job is not to just show up and complete your assigned tasks. To be a winner, to play at the top of your game, to go from an employee to an All-Star contributor, requires hard work and discipline.

One of the greatest keys to success actually starts before you make phone calls, organize a meeting, or follow up with clients. It begins by *listening*. Too often people miss this crucial step and don't pay attention to what people tell them or ask of them. We often start a job and just get busy. Weeks, months, maybe even years go by, and we assume we know what is expected of us. The danger in this is we forget to listen to what is asked of us. We miss (or ignore) the deeper questions:

- **How do I fit in my company's mission?**
- **What are my team's goals for the upcoming quarter/year?**
- **What does my team need me to do to help reach those goals?**

The Greek philosopher Epictetus once said, "We have two ears and one mouth so that we can listen twice as much as we speak." It wasn't until I learned to really listen to my coaches that I made progress. The times I resisted, made excuses, or thought I knew better were the times my game turned stagnant—or worse, regressed.

On the other hand, when I really listened to what people wanted from me, I improved my skills, enhanced my results, and increased my rate of success.

When we listen to what is expected of us, we are positioned to make informed decisions about the choices we face.

I sat down with Junior Bridgeman, CEO of Bridgeman Foods and a former Milwaukee Bucks player who made his mark in the NBA from 1975 to 1987. Just before he retired from the NBA he opened a handful of Wendy's franchises. Over the next thirty years he went on to become one of the nation's largest franchise owners, with hundreds of Wendy's and Chili's franchises, and as many as 20,000 employees.

Bridgeman was a standout player in college and was drafted by the LA Lakers, but immediately traded to Milwaukee for Kareem Abdul-Jabbar. As happens to many college stars, things changed dramatically when he arrived in the NBA. His coach, Don Nelson, sat him down and asked him to become a role player. The Bucks needed him to be their go-to sixth man, the player who doesn't start the game but is the first one off the bench to assist the team with an offensive boost.

Bridgeman said, "It was not an easy acceptance, because no one comes into the league and thinks, 'Alright, I'm going to spend my career coming off the bench, being a sixth man.'"

Nevertheless, he listened carefully and took in what his coach said he needed from him. "I had to realize that in order for the team to be successful I needed to perform this role the best that I could," admitted Bridgeman. "And in that way, I could help us all be successful. It's funny how once you accept that, you flourish."

Listening takes us to a place of better understanding and empowers us to change course if necessary. So use those "two ears" the next time you're in a company meeting, or at a get together with a key customer or family member. After you listen, there is often an opportunity to be proactive and ask questions. If speaking up intimidates you, you're not alone.

I have spoken to thousands of people, from front-line employees to executives, and without exception people say they are hesitant to ask for input and listen to feedback. When I talk about this strategy I see a physical reaction sweep across the room. Faces go from pleasant and attentive to uncomfortable and hesitant.

I get it. Most people don't want to plop down in front of the boss and ask, "So, what do you really need me to do?" We worry:

Will the boss think I have no clue how to do my job?

Will she think I've been lazy and am just now interested in doing better?

Will he point out everything I'm doing wrong and realize I shouldn't have this position?

These fears are certainly reasonable, but in reality the opposite frequently happens. By asking for input, we demonstrate that we are concerned with what our team needs; we stand out as someone willing to do what is best; we build trust; and even if we don't always like the answer, we gather information that can help us improve our performance.

Believe me, in the world of sports, when you ask a coach what you can do better, you had better pull up a chair and prepare to stay a while. The list is usually long, but that's because there is always something you can do to improve your game.

Asking questions and seeking feedback greatly enhanced my basketball career. I sought input because I knew I had a lot to learn. When I started out as a motivational speaker, I had several requests from business executives to share what I'd learned as an NBA All-Star and entrepreneur. But I wasn't a seasoned speaker.

In fact, even though I'd played in front of tens of thousands of people for more than a decade, standing in front of a large crowd alone and being expected to talk for an entire hour or more unnerved me.

Rather than assume I knew everything there was to know about speaking, I did what was natural to me. I sought out a coach to help me improve.

My speaking coach dove right in. There was no end to the list of things I had to learn to become an effective speaker. I had notes for everything from where to stand, which key words to emphasize, what facial expressions to make, to the best methods to hone my message. I didn't always enjoy it—the practice in front of mirrors, the numerous rehearsals in my car while I drove to appointments, and videotapes of myself to see how I could improve my cadence, body language, and rapport with the audience were tough. As my performance improved, however, my connection with my audiences strengthened and my ability to make a difference with my message increased.

From asking for advice from Coach Lubin in junior college, to Coach Layden and Coach Sloan at the Jazz, to my speaking coach in recent years, my life has dramatically improved because of my willingness to ask for input. I asked for and executed their expert advice to the letter.

When I spoke with my teammate Thurl Bailey, he had

a similar philosophy. "I knew basketball. It had been my craft in college. But I knew when I got to the NBA it would require another level of education. I had to be willing to learn, to ask, to absorb. Any transition has a learning curve. How long that learning curve is depends on the information you seek, and the work you put into getting better."

I fully agree. I cannot emphasize enough the *power* in asking. It does make you vulnerable, and it might mean more work and perseverance on your part, but isn't that the point? Aren't we here to improve, to contribute, to advance our skill set, and move ahead in life?

Time and time again, when I encounter companies that consistently succeed and have a workforce who thrive, the common denominator is that they gather input from their employees.

In a *Forbes* article written May 20, 2013, contributing writer Glenn Llopis said, "Listening is a leadership responsibility that does not appear in the job description. Those who do listen to their employees are in a much better position to lead the increasingly diverse and multigenerational workforce. The one-approach-fits-all way of thinking has become outdated and those who embrace the high art of listening are destined to be the better, more compassionate leaders."

Coach Jerry Sloan led the Utah Jazz for twenty-three seasons, took the team to two NBA Championship series, and finished his career with the third-most wins in NBA history (1,223). He was a listener. He had a knack for really getting to know each player. He knew where each of us excelled, where our weak spots were, and would let us know so we could understand what we needed to do to contribute to a winning season.

Coach Sloan's ability to connect with players gave him a finger on the pulse of our team. He knew the attitude each player brought to the court in any given moment. He was aware of our individual outlook, and we were aware of his desire for us to show up and play disciplined basketball. We had an open door to express our concerns and feelings to our leader. Coach Sloan made it clear our input was valued and considered. He created an environment where we had a dialogue that moved our team forward.

The willingness Coach Sloan had to engage with all of us on a deeper level created a family atmosphere that is rare and valuable in professional sports and in business.

MY SENIOR YEAR AT UCLA, when I asked Coach Lubin what I could do to make the most of the practices I had made my games, he had very specific ideas. In addition to working out six hours a day, five days a week, he prescribed that I perform 200 hook shots, 100 bank shots, 100 free throws, and 100 rim touches *daily*. Then I had to run on the track, sprinting the straightaways and walking the corners. After that, I went to the weight room and followed his workout plan to bulk up and prepare my body for the rigors of the NBA.

It was not easy, and frankly, it wasn't much fun. However, I did *exactly* what I was asked to do, day in and day out. Not something like it. I didn't do half the bank shots. I didn't cut short my time in the weight room.

A year later, as I flew to Utah to meet with Coach

Layden, I was grateful for every second I had spent in preparation, and every moment I had invested to take my skills to the next level.

In addition to asking and listening to your coach, mentor, spouse, or boss, there is someone else you should listen to as well. *You!* Ask yourself, "What can I do to improve my game? How can I increase my skills or expand my knowledge? How can I enhance my ability to contribute? How much more will I enjoy what I do if I create opportunities to get better, for no one but myself?"

When we are accountable to ourselves, when it matters to us deep down that we change and get better, things really start to change.

I experienced this during those lonely hours in the gym, relentlessly running drills. My preparation and willingness to do everything possible on my own to improve propelled me to the NBA.

The best of the best are players who spend countless hours beyond required practice time; they take shot after shot, work on agility, and go over plays repeatedly. They are the athletes focused on nutrition, who opt for fish and brown rice while others down burgers and beer after games. They are coaches who keep up on the latest developments in sports psychology and player conditioning. They are the general managers who are students of the business of the game. When all of these dedicated people converge, their teams are unstoppable!

On the other hand, countless players have the raw talent and physicality to dominate the game. They were at the top of the food chain from the time they hit puberty—from high school, college, and into the NBA. They show up to practice, put in their time, do their thing on the court, and collect their paycheck. They give the game the bare minimum. Just being who they are yields a multimillion-dollar contract. Why bust their butt to do more? Interestingly, these are the stars who fade quickly. Talent and physique alone cannot keep them at the top of the game for ten, seven, or even five years. They bounce around from team to team and their career typically ends sooner than necessary.

The choice to slide by occurs every day in business. You get the education, the job, put in your time, and collect your paycheck. Likely, you will be just fine. Perhaps you even earn a promotion. (Sadly, many unmotivated, apathetic, and incompetent people attain middle-management titles.) Too many people are guilty of just going through the motions.

Perhaps you are the exception and see every position, every role you have as an opportunity to improve; although you are not thrilled with your current entry-level job you consider it a stepping-stone. You are preparing and practicing for your chance to get more responsibility and authority. You realize that as Vince Lombardi, long-time coach of the NFL's Green Bay Packers, famously said, "Practice does not make perfect. Only perfect practice makes perfect."

If we do not practice, prepare, and learn to do things the correct way, we execute poorly at game-time. Learning first requires attention to detail; how we repeat that behavior or skill determines our success.

Personal investment and commitment pay off in more ways than those measured by statistics, raises, advancement, and awards.

Assess what you are doing to improve your game.

- **What books can you read to get better?**
- **In which training programs should you invest?**
- **What online resources can help you?**
- **Whom can you connect with to learn from their expertise?**
- **What work can you do after-hours to elevate your skills?**

The more specific your plan for improvement, the more you contribute to your team, the better positioned you will be to take on additional responsibilities and advance in your career. More important, however, is the deep satisfaction you will have in all you do.

The tire store where it all started

Shutting down Boot Bond from Pepperdine

Photo by Jayne Kamin / LA Times

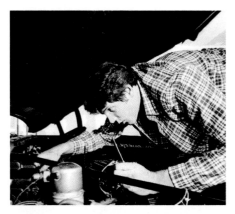

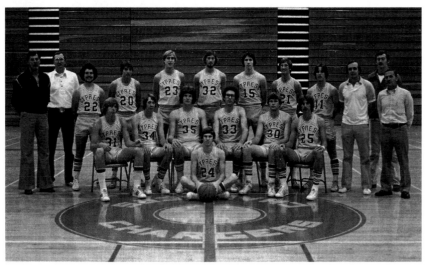

1980 Cypress College State Championship Team

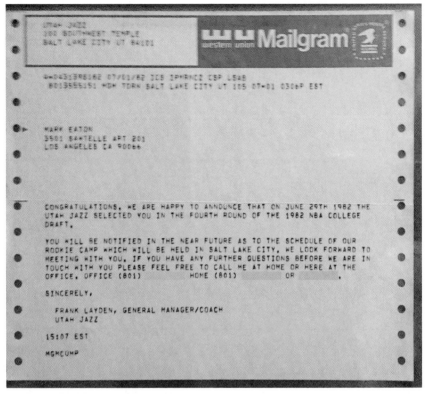

Mailgram— the old-school way to find out you have been drafted.

Midwest Division Champions, the 1983-84 Utah Jazz team hit all the right notes.

Mark Eaton and Magic Johnson

Photo by Al Hartmann / SL Tribune Staff

Photo by Sporting News via Getty Images

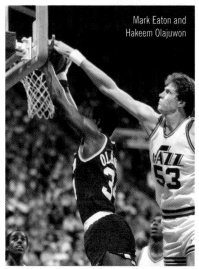

Mark Eaton and Hakeem Olajuwon

Photo by Focus on Sport / Getty Images

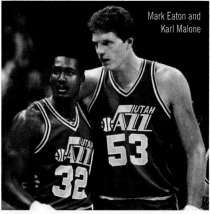

Mark Eaton and Karl Malone

Photo by Sporting News via Getty Images

Mark Eaton and John Stockton

Mark Eaton and Michael Jordan

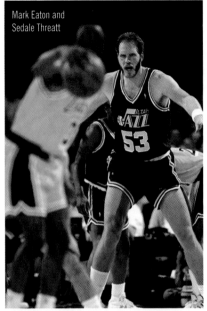

Mark Eaton and
Sedale Threatt

Mark Eaton and
Patrick Ewing

Photo by Andrew D. Bernstein / NBAE via Getty Images

Photo by Andrew D. Bernstein / NBAE via Getty Images

Mark Eaton and
Olden Polynice

Mark Eaton and
Hakeem Olajuwon

Photo by Jon Soohoo / NBAE via Getty Images

Photo by Bill Baptist / NBAE via Getty Images

1989 All-Stars, Mark Eaton, John Stockton, and Karl Malone

Photo by Norm Perdue / Utah Jazz photographer

Mark Eaton with Robert Parish and Larry Bird

Photo by Dick Raphael / NBAE via Getty Images

Photo by Focus on Sport / Getty Images

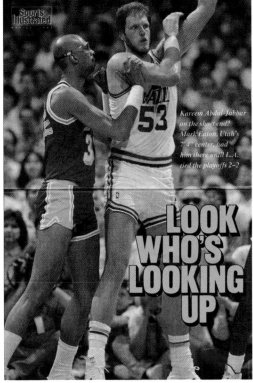

Kareem Abdul-Jabbar on the short end? Mark Eaton, Utah's 7'4" center, had him there until L.A. tied the playoffs 2–2

LOOK WHO'S LOOKING UP

Photo by Peter Read Miller / Sports Illustrated / Getty Images

Mark Eaton and John Stockton

Photo by John W. McDonough / Sports Illustrated / Getty Images

NBA 1989 All-Star Team, West

Photo by Andrew D. Bernstein/NBAE via Getty Images

Photo by Andrew D. Bernstein / NBAE via Getty Images

Photo by Salt Lake Tribune staff photographer

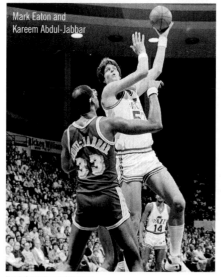

Mark Eaton and
Kareem Abdul-Jabbar

Photo by Sporting News via Getty Images

Photo by Andrew D. Bernstein / NBAE via Getty Images

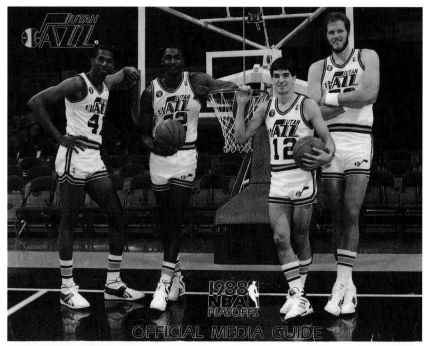

Photo by Norm Perdue / Utah Jazz photographer

Mark Eaton and Otis Thorpe

Photo by Bill Baptist / NBAE via Getty Images

Mark Eaton with Coach Sloan

Photo by Jeffrey Allred / Deseret News

Jerry Sloan's Jersey Retirement Ceremony, L to R: Karl Malone, Trainer Don "Sparky" Sparks, Bryon Russell, Hot Rod Hundley, Thurl Bailey, John Stockton, Coach Frank Layden, Mark Eaton, Coach Jerry Sloan, Scott Layden, John Crotty

2014 Reunion of 1984 Midwest Division Champion Team, L to R: Coach Phil Johnson, Jerry Eaves, Thurl Bailey, Head Coach Frank Layden, Mark Eaton, Rich Kelley, Dave Checketts, Darrell Griffith

Mark & Teri Eaton

Mark receiving the Man of the Year Award for Cypress College in 2014. L to R: Head Coach Don Johnson, Mark Eaton, Swen Nater, Assistant Coaches Jack Long and Tom Lubin

Delivering a big message in Texas   Photo by David Barrett

Coach Tom Lubin and Mark

Mark and his horse, Big Tim, take a swimming lesson
Photo by Tom Smart

CHAPTER 7

"I've got a theory that if you give 100% all of the time, somehow things will work out in the end."

- LARRY BIRD

B Y THE END OF THE SUMMER OF 1982, I had left UCLA and a coach who had never seen my value behind. The Utah Jazz had drafted me, but late in the fourth round. While being drafted is exciting, it does not guarantee membership on the team that drafts you. It gives you, in essence, an audition, a tryout. You have to prove your worth and earn your position on the squad, just as I had done in the summer league games. I had done it before, and I would do it again.

To prepare myself to play in the NBA, I continued to work out with Coach Lubin and play in the LA summer league. Coach Layden came to California to watch me and said, "I like what I see. I can tell you have been working hard. You're a little rough around the edges. If you want to come to our training camp a month early, put in extra work with the coaches and get on our weight training program, this just might work."

There was no question in my mind; I would give the

team all I had. I showed up in Utah nervous, anxious, and excited. I *was* rather concerned when I realized I was the *only* player asked to come early. The pressure was intense. In time, however, I recognized the incredible benefit I received from having the laser focus of the entire coaching staff. Though much of our court banter and lunchtime conversations were about their game philosophy, I also talked to the coaches about life in general. I got to know them, and they really got to know me.

It was a challenging time. The coaches put together a game plan to get their 7'4" prospect ready to play in the NBA. They were serious about training and so was I. Scott Layden (Frank's son and an assistant coach) met me at Sugarhouse Park every day to run in Utah's hundred-degree heat. Phil Johnson met me at the gym for hours of relentless drills.

And, it all paid off. Coach Layden initially had a three-year plan to develop me into a starting center. A few months into our season, however, starting center Danny Schayes was traded to the Denver Nuggets. Suddenly, I was thrust into the role of starting center of the Utah Jazz. I continued to listen to the coaches and do exactly what they asked of me, and ended up with a solid rookie season—275 blocked shots in 81 games (a franchise record). That performance ranked me third in the NBA for blocked shots, behind Atlanta's Wayne "Tree" Rollins and San Diego's Bill Walton.

Fortunately, as I followed the game plan, I continued to grow and improve in my role as a defender. Sadly, it does not always work so well. Sometimes you follow a game plan perfectly and still do not achieve the desired results. That is what happened to our team in the first round of the 1987 NBA playoffs.

A basic principle every competitive athlete learns is not to fuel the fire of your opponent. Never provide them with extra incentive to beat you. That extra incentive can come in the form of an inflammatory remark or quote, an obvious lack of respect, or in our case, a fight.

The energy in the Salt Palace was electric as we played the Golden State Warriors. It was the second game in the series. We had played really well and had the Warriors on the ropes. We were ahead at the end of the game and virtually assured a win. If we prevailed in this game, we would only need one more victory to win the series. No team in decades had come back from a two-game deficit in a best-of-five series.

As the final seconds ticked off the clock, Karl Malone and Greg Ballard from the Warriors got tangled up. Malone took exception to this and threw the ball at Ballard, who then caught the ball and threw it back at Malone's head. The teams broke into an all-out brawl. The fracas continued back and forth across the court, and culminated in the Warriors' coach, George Karl, exchanging punches with a Jazz fan. It was an ugly scene.

The referees and security eventually gained control and sent both teams to the locker room. We still had a lead in the series, but we had awakened the sleeping Warriors giant, and we paid the price for it.

The fight between Malone and Ballard galvanized the

Warriors and their fans. We traveled to Oakland to play games three and four where a transformed team greeted us. We walked into a sold-out arena.

We lost games three and four on the Warriors' home court, then returned to Salt Lake and lost game five on our home court as well. We became the first team since 1956 to lose a series after a two-game lead.

After the final game, the Warriors' players credited the fight to stoking their fire. In an interview, Eric "Sleepy" Floyd said the fight "keyed our comeback. We have to thank Malone for that. He gave us the motivation when he hit Ballard with the ball. They had the game won. If Malone had just walked off the court, we would have walked off kind of down because we had lost."

Karl Malone is an impeccable athlete and a sharp, levelheaded player who did not typically give in to moments such as that. Nor, as a rule, did our team participate in on-court fights. It is a great example that even the best player on the best team can get off-track and forget the game plan. Failure to stick to protocol, deviation from the game plan, and a disregard for the needs of the group are all variations of one simple problem: poor execution. It often occurs when we do what we think is best, what is easiest, or what we feel like doing.

These brief lapses can have devastating consequences. In our case, it cost us the season.

Sometimes, poor execution occurs when we only focus on things that are easily tracked and documented. In the NBA, that shows up as a focus on the parts of your job that show up in the stats columns. While great stats are commendable, there are times we are required to focus on aspects of the job not noticed by the press or fans. I knew this as well as anyone.

I had my share of fans and supporters, but I also had numerous detractors who felt I did not do my part offensively for our team. Those people, however, were not in our team practices. I was clear on what our coaches expected of me, and I focused on the execution of those expectations. While my detractors fixated on my offensive stats, my supporters and coaches understood and appreciated the overall impact I had on the games. The way I executed my job influenced our opponents' offense, game plan, and their shooting percentage. Some Jazz fans complained about my lack of speed and scoring. However, our opponents complained they had to adjust their shots and strategy when they faced me on the court. I did what I was asked to do and influenced our opponents' performance in a way that helped our team win games.

If I had only focused on the aspects of my job that fans cared most about, I would not have executed my role. Poor execution would have led to more losses.

Loss of business from poor execution can be devastating in many areas. Even if a company has a stellar operations team and product development approach, if employees do not execute their tasks well, they cause a company to lose sales and impede the company's overall success. If improving the company and its bottom line is not incentive enough to avoid poor execution, perhaps self-preservation is.

Over the past several years, I have delivered hundreds of presentations on teamwork to a wide variety of industries. A mistake in execution for many of these companies—manufacturers, transportation, construction, and energy, can result in the loss of a limb, mobility, or even life. According to the AFL-CIO, a voluntary federation of 56 national and international labor unions, more than 4,500 American workers lost their lives on the job in 2013 alone.

For many of the groups I work with, workplace safety is a priority. My client Doug Sterbenz, past executive vice president and COO for Westar Energy, said his company worked hard to bring safety to the forefront. "We have helped employees see safety as part of their job, every bit as much as keeping the lights on or repairing a downed line," he said. "We explained if they do the job, but they don't do it safely, they're not actually doing their job."

AN EMPLOYEE'S POOR PERFORMANCE is a common reason for being fired. When an employee consistently fails to carry out stated objectives or guidelines there is frequently no option but to let them go. Players and employees often understand the company game plan and their role in it, but for whatever reason choose not to do it, or don't do it to the best of their ability. They may be asked to do something difficult or challenging; something that takes sacrifice like working longer hours, or something that stretches their abilities and makes them uncomfortable. Whatever the reason, when they ignore the game plan, the effectiveness of the entire group is affected.

John Stockton was a team player who knew that when he followed the game plan he would have to do the dirty work many players didn't want to do.

At six feet tall, Stockton was often on the floor with players who were a foot taller than he was and much stronger. As part of our offense, he was called on to set screens (obstruct his teammate's defender to free him up to score) underneath the basket where the big men played. It's a tough job to set a screen on a player who outweighs you by a hundred pounds. Many guards in the NBA want no part of that assignment. They make a half-hearted effort or no effort at all, as they venture into the key.

There is no spot on a stat sheet that tallies screens set by a player; it's a job that comes with no praise and a lot of bruises. Stockton embraced this assignment and even relished it as he became an irritant to the big men who didn't like him to set screens at their waistlines. I can still see him staunchly setting his feet, bracing himself, arms up, elbows out like a football player, getting ready to take the full force of the other team's big man as he tried to stop Karl Malone from scoring a goal.

Stockton was tough as nails and I loved to watch him work. Coach Sloan emphasized toughness in the huddle by saying, "Go lay some meat on somebody." Stockton would happily do just that. He sacrificed his body and freed up his teammates to score.

DAVE CHECKETTS relayed another great example of following a game plan. Checketts is a fixture in the NBA, NHL, Major League Soccer, TV networks, and many other sports-related ventures as an owner, president, and general manager. I got to know him when, at age 28, he became the general manager and president of the Jazz—the youngest executive in NBA history. From the Jazz, he went on to become the president of the New York Knicks, and eventually the president and CEO of Madison Square Garden. While he was at the helm, the New York Knicks made it to the Eastern Conference Finals three times and the NBA Finals twice.

During the 1998 season, the Knicks were in need of a star player to help them reach the finals. The Knicks' coach, Jeff Van Gundy, and general manager, Ernie Grunfeld, pushed Checketts hard to consider signing star player Latrell Sprewell. Sprewell had had serious problems on and off the court. His most recent problem had been a one-year suspension from the NBA after he attacked and choked his coach in practice! Checketts said the only way he would sign Sprewell was if he could sit down and interview him. Van Gundy, Grunfeld, and Checketts went to Sprewell's house and talked to him for four hours. Then Checketts asked if he could talk to Sprewell alone.

Checketts was blunt. "I said, 'Look, we don't know each other, but I'm about to make a decision that could bring you to New York and put you on the biggest stage in the world, Madison Square Garden. If you come and play the way I know you are capable of playing, you will resurrect your career. I mean it's dead right now, but you have a coach and general manager who want you. What assurances do I have that we won't have to put up with a circus?'"

Sprewell said, "I want this opportunity. I want to show what I'm capable of, and you have my word that I will not create a single problem for you. I promise: not a single problem."

Checketts decided to give him a chance. Sprewell was sincere about wanting to redeem himself, and the only way to do that was to follow the roadmap Checketts gave him.

After signing Sprewell, the Knicks went on a run and made it all the way to the NBA Finals. Although they came up short, Sprewell averaged 26 points a game in the series, and as Checketts told me, "If we had somehow won the championship, he would have been the MVP." Better yet, "He was never late. He never said anything amiss to the press. He had something to prove, and we provided him an environment to do that."

In the NBA, I had the opportunity to see, firsthand, the importance and impact of a great game plan. As I mentioned earlier, I served as a player rep for the NBA Players Association, the union established to negotiate everything from salaries to benefits for the players. In that role, I spent time with David Stern, who served as NBA Commissioner for more than three decades and is lauded for his vision, business acumen, and bold leadership style.

When the NBA hired Stern in 1978, he was employee number 24. At that time, most games aired on tape-delay, if they aired at all. The league generated around $100 million in annual revenue. Stern took the league from obscurity to international prominence. Under his leadership, the NBA grew by seven franchises and launched the WNBA and NBA Developmental League. Today the global entity employs more than 1,200 people, has *billions* of viewers around the world via television and digital media, and generates six *billion* dollars in annual revenue.

This feat is even more impressive when you understand what he was up against when he first brought the NBA owners, general managers, and players together. The owners were generally billionaires, used to running their own show and unaccustomed to answering to others. The general managers were there to make things work for the owner and the players. The players' priorities were game time, pay, benefits, and playing time. Throw in the advertisers, who expected a great product (exciting NBA games) and big results (high viewership that translated into increased revenue), and it's obvious what a gigantic task Stern had on his hands.

I asked David how he faced the monumental challenges of the early days, and brought so many groups with different agendas together to work toward common goals. He explained that before he arrived, each team did their own thing. There were huge salary disparities among the large and small markets. If a team wanted to televise games in a foreign country, they went right ahead and did so, without anyone else's permission. If they decided to create a promotional video, they shot whatever they wanted.

The budget-strapped Jazz, for example, created a regrettably unforgettable sponsor video. It featured our hefty coach, Frank Layden, cigar in mouth and wearing a T-shirt with a body-builder's six-pack image on the front, running on the shores of the Great Salt Lake to the soundtrack from

Chariots of Fire. Funny? Yes. Great production value? Well, that is questionable.

For Stern, it was imperative to unify and elevate the NBA brand and manage its growth. He created a distinct brand identity, developed a strategy for everything from television exposure to public service, and asked every team to adhere to the guidelines. He said, "My focus in the early years was developing a presence for the team—the NBA was the team—and determining how to make it grow, together. Because if we did that as a whole, each of the individual NBA teams would do well. I was fiercely protective, because I came out of a legal background and I considered the NBA to be my client. I was going to protect it and help it to grow."

He did exactly that. Before long, the teams bought into his vision. They followed the league game plan and paved the way for the NBA's exponential growth.

When we follow the given game plan we put the team, and the individual, in position to succeed. It is not rocket science. No one needs to reinvent the wheel. The key to Commitment #2 is simple: Follow the game plan. When you are assigned a new project or your company launches a new initiative, jump in and do what you are asked to do.

IT REQUIRES TIME AND EFFORT to carry a game plan to fruition. In sports, that translates to long hours spent training, conditioning, practicing, and drilling.

I think many people assume that elite players have such extraordinary natural athletic ability that they don't have to put in much practice. That is just not the case. What separates the very best players from the good players is plain old-fashioned hard work.

Many players in the NBA take the summer off and put on weight. They use training camp as the time to get in shape for the season. Not my teammates! Karl Malone and John Stockton always came into camp in game shape so they were able to focus on other aspects of their game during camp. Our team had a competitive edge to begin the season because of their dedication.

Their commitment to fitness had a huge effect on our team. Eventually every player showed up for training camp in game shape, ready to play.

Another player who always exceeded expectations, despite his superstar status, was Larry Bird. Bird played for the Boston Celtics from 1979 to 1992, and was part of one of the greatest teams in the NBA. He was a twelve-time NBA All-Star, won three NBA championships, and was the league's Most Valuable Player three consecutive times.

Every time we played the Celtics, we knew we were in for a battle. They played in the Boston Garden, one of the most storied and historic venues in the NBA. It was actually an old, rundown facility, but it looked great on TV. Because of the Garden mystique and the Celtic franchise history (seventeen championships over the years) just stepping into the building felt a little overwhelming and intimidating. Once inside the arena, we would look up at the rafters, see the numerous NBA championship banners, and be awed.

The venue was not the only thing that impressed me when we played the Celtics. We typically arrived at the arena around four p.m., several hours before the game. As we made our way to the locker room, we would peer through the portals out to the court. Without fail, we saw Larry Bird, one of the best players in the NBA, shooting jumpers by himself.

I learned a lot from players like Bird, who worked hard to exceed expectations. They were the players determined to go beyond being good; they accepted nothing less than greatness.

Exceeding expectations is something Coach Lubin introduced me to at Cypress College and continued to reinforce when I went to UCLA. It was hard for me, as a twenty-one-year-old, to put in so much time before, during, and after practice. It wasn't easy to follow the coaches' regimens, the exhaustive conditioning, and the endless drills. It was even more difficult in light of the fact that I still sat the bench most of my time as a Bruin.

Ever patient, Coach Lubin reminded me the work was about the future, not the present. I had to do all that was asked of me, and a little bit more, to achieve that future.

My focus on Commitment #2, **Do What You're Asked to Do**, enabled me to exceed the expectations of the Jazz management, coaching staff, and myself as well. When I joined the team, I believed I would be the back-up center and play ten minutes a game. However, because I did what was asked of me, I became the starting center just months into my first season—a position I held until my retirement twelve seasons later. I became the league leader in blocked shots my *second* year.

If you want to become an All-Star in your industry, start by doing what you're asked to do. Listen when people tell you what is expected of you. Communicate your game plan. Ask if there is anything you should be more focused on or doing differently. Then follow the game plan, and exceed expectations.

QUESTIONS & EXERCISES

On a piece of paper or on your computer, write down the answers to the following questions.

- Are you clear about what your boss expects of you?

- Are you clear about what the members of your team expect of you?

- Are you clear about what other departments in your company expect of you?

- Are you clear about what your customer expects of you?

- On a scale from 1 to 10, how well do you execute the requests of others?

- How can knowing what others need from you make your job easier?

COMMITMENT #3

MAKE PEOPLE LOOK GOOD

CHAPTER 8

"One man can be a crucial ingredient on a team,
but one man cannot make a team."

- KAREEM ABDUL-JABBAR

So far we have focused on the importance of personal performance and individual execution. Team success, however, requires more than concentrated personal effort. The third commitment requires making people look good. This is an undervalued aspect of team and personal success in the world today.

When we make it part of our job to make our teammates look good, the success of our team is enhanced. The screens John Stockton set for me did not show up on his personal stats sheet, but they assisted me, and others, in improving our stats and made us look good.

By 1986, I had been with the Jazz for four years. Coach Layden had worked tirelessly to change our mentality from an unconnected group of individual players accustomed to losing to a cohesive team who believed they could win.

Our record had improved, but that did not mean every game went well, and every loss took its toll. After one of those painful defeats, I witnessed something I will never forget.

We were in the middle of a series of back-to-back games, and our next opponent was the Sacramento Kings. We lost the first game, but one of our key players had a great night. He scored over 30 points and had double-digit rebounds. After the game, while the rest of us were down and frustrated in the locker room, he was ecstatic. He strutted around the locker room with a huge smile on this face, joking with everyone. He could not have been more proud of his performance.

We returned home and faced Sacramento on our home court the next night. This same player had a mediocre night statistically but we won the game. Afterwards, the locker room was electric. We all celebrated our victory and had a great time, but this player sat by himself in the corner with his head down in defeat.

The general manager of the Jazz visited the locker room after both of these games and saw the player's behavior firsthand. Not long after this blatant display of selfishness, management traded him to another team.

I use that example not to say one shouldn't have personal goals. On the contrary, I believe it is natural, and important, to focus on personal achievement. Everyone does. What I am saying is problems arise, and people around us suffer, when we focus *only* on ourselves.

Today, more than ever, our culture seems driven by thoughts of "me first." It permeates nearly every facet of our lives. We strive for the next job, the promotion, the corner office, and all the trappings—the car, the house, the clothes, the technology—that say to the world, "Look at me, I'm a success!" Then we post it all on social media. This cultural drive to get individual attention can often cause us to sacrifice the greater good for our own advancement or accolades.

In basketball, we refer to attention-seekers as black holes. Simply stated, a black hole is the player who stops the ball. Once they receive the ball from a teammate, it will not come back. Every time they touch the ball, they shoot. They may be talented players who put up incredible stats, but they care more about those stats than winning or losing. They focus so intently on their own game, they forget there are four other players on the court.

When you play as a team, the ball moves from player to player in an effort to get the best possible shot. The Golden State Warriors have been an ideal example of this. They move the ball until the right shot is open. In contrast, black holes disrupt or stop movement. They cause contention, doubt, second-guessing, and decline in morale.

Black holes are not only the players who hog the ball. They are also the players on the bench who complain, criticize and second-guess the coach, stay seated during time-outs, and try to get others to join in their frustration. I admit it was tough to ignore them sometimes, but I had come too far and learned too much about the value of teamwork to join in their grumblings.

A black hole can be present in any environment or workplace. Sometimes black holes are incredibly talented people who grab the attention, take all the credit, or simply do not work well with others. They do not seem to realize their success is due, in part, to the group of people who created the product or provided back-end support for them. They forget there is an entire system that comes together to give them the opportunity to shine.

Other times black holes drain a company of productive energy and team spirit. They can be a boss, a salesperson, someone in the next cubicle, or the gang at the water cooler who gripes about management and backstabs colleagues.

I recently consulted with a healthcare CEO. With the changes to healthcare rules and regulations over the past few years, the industry has experienced seismic shifts. My client talked at length about his struggle with a fellow member of the management team, a sales executive who had always been a top performer but now suffered significant struggles closing new business.

When the management group tried to work with him, and encouraged him to make the necessary adjustments to become more of a team player, he vehemently resisted. Eventually the company had to let this former top performer go because he refused to adapt to a changing marketplace. The black hole he created was toxic. With his departure, and a few other changes, the company drew together as a team and sales soared.

It's a common problem. Most CEOs and managers tell me their biggest struggle does not come from outside competition. Rather it is the *internal* competition—the pettiness, infighting, and lack of cohesion among their own employees—that causes the most grief.

Sci-fi movies often show a frantic space crew as they desperately try to avoid the dreaded black hole. We watch in anticipation as they do everything they can to skirt disaster. The music crescendos as the ship draws closer and closer to the universe's greatest vortex, unavoidably pulled in by its gravitational force. The audience knows if the ship goes in, the crew will never come out.

When an employee or manager causes that kind of pull, they can be just as much of a threat. Selfishness in the workplace destroys morale, corrupts company culture, and encourages an every man for himself attitude, the opposite of collaboration and teamwork.

Gravitational pull, black hole syndrome—it all boils down to a sole focus on one's own needs and a disregard for the needs of the team. I talked with a friend who shared how her boss, who was a great manager in many ways, had a tendency to go "black hole" in one aspect of the business. By departmental design, my friend and her colleagues did the lion's share of the workload. With direction from their boss, they researched, designed the concept, and wrote the final presentation. When it came time for the client pitch, however, they watched as their boss took credit for all the work.

His behavior bothered the team greatly, but they felt powerless to stop it since he was the boss. Over time his habit of hogging the limelight without mention of their efforts took its toll. Many of the employees moved on and found positions where their contributions were acknowledged and appreciated.

Dave Checketts shared a story from his first year as president of the New York Knicks that illustrates the point as well. Checketts was new to the team, and so was Coach Pat Riley, who had left the LA Lakers, where he had been named Coach of the Year. Checketts wanted to put together a special event to celebrate the start of the new season. He said, "I wanted the team to feel like good things were ahead. I went to our catering crew at Madison Square Garden. I said, 'Look, I want to make this a great lunch, plenty to eat, the best steaks, the best lobster. We're going to treat them as royalty, because they've been beaten up by the New York press for a few years.' So we had a special luncheon, and it was a great event," he continued. "Our catering crew just did a phenomenal job. Then I got the bill. I figured out that meal cost me over $1,000 a person!"

Checketts was flabbergasted. While the catering team had done a fabulous job, he could have gone to New York's finest restaurant, ordered everything on the menu, and spent less. He called the head of facilities for an explanation, as he felt there had to be a mistake. Checketts said the response from the head of facilities was, "Dave, I'm sorry, but you've got to understand I need to hit my numbers!" He was so narrowly focused he only worried about his department making their numbers, even though it cost the company as a whole.

Checketts said that was his first lesson in how things worked at Madison Square Garden: Everyone looked out for his or her own bottom line. Over the next few years, he saw that myopic attitude play out among all of the sister companies, which included the New York Knicks, New York Rangers, New York Liberty, Madison Square Garden arena, and the MSG Television Network. He said he hated to admit it, but he eventually found himself doing the same: protecting the Knicks' needs over everyone else's. "I did my fair share to create discontent among the divisions, because it was always a battle," he explained.

This "my group first" attitude is all too common. No business is immune to this way of thinking. I have seen it erode small companies and large corporations.

To consider the needs of others, as well as our own, can be difficult. However, when we do, we are positioned for greater success. Dave watched the bitterness fester in every department for the three years he served as the Knicks' president. When he was promoted to president and CEO of Madison Square Garden, he commissioned a study from a consulting company to explore employee satisfaction. "After the consultants had been in and interviewed everybody in the company, this was the final line of their report: *'This company is the most mean-spirited company we have ever encountered. We can't believe how much hate there is.'*"

Wow!

Checketts knew he had to turn the culture from one of competition to one of cooperation. "As CEO, the first thing I did was change everybody's compensation," he said. "Instead of making 100% of their bonus conditional on hitting their own budgets, I made it so that 90% of their bonus was dependent upon the company making its goals. It was incredible how it changed people's perspective."

He organized weekly meetings for all the division heads where they would bring up problems and work on them before they festered. He implemented off-site meetings to bring in various team managers and MSG Network representatives to work together. He said the improved collaboration and communal compensation plan "turned the network into a big cheerleader for the club. Instead of being fodder for the New York press, they were actually positive about us. The place became a different place to work over those years. People really came together. It started by changing compensation to reflect a team mentality. You only succeed when the team succeeds."

I know this for a fact. When we make the transition to a team-centered approach, we prepare for the win-win. We are poised for greater success when we make others look good. As a 7'4" center who wasn't the fastest runner or the best shooter on the court, I made a career out of helping others so our team could succeed. As I helped my teammates shine, I unexpectedly found a place in the spotlight too. This is the embodiment of Commitment #3, *Make People Look Good.*

CHAPTER 9

"Create unselfishness as the most important team attribute."

- BILL RUSSELL

WHEN I STARTED MY CAREER with the Jazz in 1982, the team was in dire straits. We were not winning much on the court. Off the court, our struggles were even worse. Things hit rock bottom when Coach Layden, who was also the general manager at the time, got a call from our team owner, Sam Battistone. He told Layden the team needed a million dollars in order to make payroll on Monday, and he wondered if Layden had any ideas on how to come up with the money. The only thing Layden could think of was to trade the Jazz's number three overall pick, Dominique Wilkins, whom the Jazz had drafted a few months earlier. He was an outstanding player out of Georgia who was sure to become an NBA All-Star. However, the Jazz needed immediate money to make payroll, so Layden called the Atlanta Hawks and offered up Wilkins for a million dollars in cash. The Hawks obviously jumped at the opportunity and threw a couple of utility players into the deal.

In this financially tumultuous time for the Jazz, our struggles on the court were just as real. Wins were rare, and so was team unity. Coach Layden was determined to change the culture of our team. Prior to his arrival, the team had grown accustomed to losing. There were frequent trades and a revolving door of players. Players punched the time clock, showed up for the game, put up their fifteen shots, and went home. There was a lot of selfish play. We had become what many losing teams become: a group of individuals only concerned about their own success.

Coach Layden initiated our transformation. He taught us to "stop competing with each other and start cooperating with each other." He promised that if we did this, the individual accolades would show up. "Here's how we will do it: We're going to play defense first. We are not going to try to outscore the other team. We will focus on defense and then we are going to run the ball, and score on opportunities that we create—either by blocking a shot, getting a steal, or creating a deflection."

He asked us to focus on smaller, achievable goals that would help us become a better, more cohesive team. For example, he would say, "If we're not going to be in the playoffs, we are going to affect the playoffs. Focus on beating the better teams out there." So we gunned for the Lakers, Celtics, and Sixers. Over time, our play improved and we held our own against them and, eventually, we beat them!

Coach Layden said, "I'd rather lose a game by two points than three, because two points is closer to winning." His unique viewpoint and innovative ideas altered our focus. We started to understand that we were no longer just a group of individuals. We started to believe in each other and play as a team, and as a result, our culture transformed. Our attitude became "Hey, we can do this, we can win games!" After we beat the Celtics and the Lakers, the fans really got excited and they, too, began to believe in us.

From there, every player bought into the culture of winning. We began to understand that a commitment to the concept of being a team, to pass the ball and help our teammates, benefited us personally as well. Camaraderie blossomed and friendships were forged that endure to this day. And it was *fun*!

Just as Coach Layden predicted, the individual accolades rolled in as our team play improved. The next season we made the playoffs and won the division for the first time in team history. In addition, I led the NBA in blocked shots, Adrian Dantley led the NBA in scoring, Rickey Green led the NBA in steals, and Darrell Griffith led the NBA in 3-point shooting. This was an unheard-of feat, especially impressive considering our dismal history.

Over the next two years, the team drafted John Stockton and Karl Malone and the culture of teamwork continued to thrive. Our success was built on hard work, extra passes, tough defense, and running the ball on opportunity. It was our road map to winning. At the same time players started to make more money, ticket sales went up, and there was much more interest in our team. Everyone benefited—both individually and collectively—because we were all intent on making others look good.

The assist is one of the ways we made each other look good. Typically, the player who scores the most is the one fans notice. A skilled player can certainly score on his own, but with a great assist or great pass, his job is made easier.

One goal of a team is to find the simplest way to score. If your teammate has a better opportunity to score than you do, your job is to get them the ball. Most often your teammate will acknowledge you when you do this. However, whether or not you are acknowledged or appreciated by your teammate, teamwork has to start somewhere. It has to start with you.

One of my favorite examples of an assist is the outlet pass. The greatest feeling I had on the basketball court was initiating the fast break—quickly moving the ball down the floor for an easy score. When the opposing team missed a shot, it was my job to collect the rebound, keep the ball high, and quickly find John Stockton near half court to start a fast break. The faster I got him the ball, the better chance he had to push the ball up the floor and hit a streaking Karl Malone for an easy goal or slam-dunk. The feeling when that happened was euphoric, and we achieved our team goal—scoring.

The assist is a powerful example of the synergy required for team success. It requires the commitment to do whatever it takes to come together and execute as a team on every play. When you pass the ball to another player, you need to know his preferences—how he wants the ball, where he wants the ball, and what he likes to do with the ball when he gets it. When you are in the zone you have an automatic sense of where the other players are on the floor; you can feel where the defense is and you know exactly where to throw the ball.

Like John Stockton, Pete Maravich had an incredible knack for knowing exactly where to put the ball to help make the play. Maravich, who played for the Atlanta Hawks, Utah Jazz, and Boston Celtics, was a five-time NBA All-Star and played from 1970 to 1980. Nicknamed Pistol Pete for his gun-slinging style of play, he was widely known for his ability to put up points—he averaged over 24 points per game in the NBA. He was also the kind of player who made others look good.

If you watch footage from Maravich's career, you see his uncanny ability to deliver the ball at the right moment, with a finesse not typically seen in passing. Usually a player fires the ball to get it where it needs to be. Amazingly, even when Maravich was running full-speed, he could throw floater passes that landed softly in the hands of his teammate. It was as if the ball was suspended in time waiting for his teammate to receive it. It was that precise. While he had a stellar ten-year run, his failing knees called for the end of his career. Maravich played his final season in Boston with then-rookie Larry Bird. Despite his joint trouble, he was still a great contributor and helped the Celtics earn the best record in the league that year.

I challenge you to discover how to use the power of the assist to make others look good in your workplace or home. How can you make your boss feel like a success? Is she a detail-oriented leader who wants to be kept in the loop by meticulous reports? Is he a big-picture manager who would rather let you loose and get general updates down the road? What about your colleagues? What helps them shine? Have you ever stepped in to help them finish a project or provide back-up support? It feels great, doesn't it? What about your spouse, partner, or a family member? How can you best assist them?

When we gain an understanding of those around us and find specific ways to help them get ahead, we create an atmosphere of collaboration that helps everyone. The effect is contagious. So go ahead, start an epidemic of making people look good!

CHAPTER 10

"Ask not what your teammates can do for you. Ask what you can do for your teammates."

- MAGIC JOHNSON

ATHLETES ARE TRAINED to ask for and receive feedback, advice, and criticism from coaches. Any time we lace up our shoes or cleats we are told what we did right, what we did wrong, and what we need to do to improve. Constructive criticism and constant coaching is part of being on a team.

The best players embrace this. They don't take it personally, and they learn from their coaches. They ask what they can do better and they consistently practice what it is they have been coached to do.

Although many of us have played sports at some level, in a business setting it's often more difficult to get feedback from our boss or peers. We don't have the same desire to be advised, coached, and instructed. Most of us fear criticism and advice. It makes us feel inadequate, like we're doing something wrong, or in danger of losing our job.

You can change that paradigm. It's a matter of perspective. See your boss as a coach who does her job, in part, because she wants you to get better—she wants you and your team to succeed. She wants you to win.

Trust me, in my experience as a business owner and speaker for corporations, I have learned it is common for employees to dread negative feedback, fear employer reviews, or believe the boss hates them or wants to fire them if they hear any criticism. People avoid asking for input because if they hear something negative it makes them feel "less-than," not up to par.

My CAREER TOOK OFF when I embraced the advice of my coaches. It wasn't easy to hear the criticism, even when I knew it was given so I could improve my skills. It stung on occasion; sometimes it even made my blood boil. I inwardly cringed when Coach Lubin gave me a long list of things to fix. Early on when Coach Layden pulled me aside to deliver some "finer points," I struggled not to voice a retort.

I believe the sports adage: If the coach isn't yelling at you or asking you to improve, worry because it means he's given up on you or plans to play somebody else. This applies to every aspect of life. While it is not pleasant to hear you should do better at something, the reality is *you can always do better.* When your boss, coach, or spouse points that out, take it as a good sign that they are engaged in your personal development, and thank them!

This powerful—if simple—piece of advice is invaluable: Don't be afraid to hear feedback on how you can do your job better. Encourage it. Ask for it. It will help you reach your career goals, team goals, and life goals. Don't make assumptions that you are doing what you are supposed to be doing or doing the task correctly. Ask your boss, your colleagues, your spouse, your friends, and those you interact with what you can do to make them look good. Their answer may surprise and enlighten you.

Whether through humor or another style of communication, sincerely asking how you can help others succeed can be a career-changing experience. It can put you in a position to make a lasting difference.

Recognize that you cannot just sit down in a chair and haphazardly ask an open-ended question like, "So, what do you want me to do to help you look better?"

You have to be strategic. Start by sharing the details of what you are currently doing with your boss or team. *Then* ask if there is anything you can do differently or additionally to help your boss or your colleagues achieve their objectives.

It is important to touch base with your boss and other colleagues often to ensure you are on the same page, otherwise it's easy to get off course. You can fall into the trap of busy work, tending to things you might think are important, but that do not serve the goals of the team.

For example, in basketball you can run plays all day long, but if nobody scores, those plays don't make a difference. If you don't progress toward a goal, you won't win. If you are not advancing, it is time to change the play.

Fortunately, in basketball you always know if your action—the play you choose, the pass you make, or the bucket you shoot—is the right one; you just look to the scoreboard for immediate confirmation. In business, however, there's no real-time scoreboard. The only way to get the information you need is to ask.

It is far better to ask than assume you are doing a great job. Never be in a position where you wish you had asked for clear direction about expectations and opportunities.

ONCE YOU KNOW what others need to help them succeed, go back to Commitment #2—*Do What You're Asked to Do*. Don't do what you *think* is best. Instead, listen to what you've been asked, then, do it! Period.

Then ask yourself: How, exactly, will I get this done? How will I know I've made progress? Are there benchmarks to attain? What is my goal? How will it be measured?

Some people see the act of helping others as being extraordinary. I would contend it is not, it just seems that way to those who don't do it. In the world of teamwork it's exactly what's required. In basketball, you have to help others fulfill their role on the court. In your career, you will fare better when you execute the company's business plan and help others do the same.

Adopting Commitment #3, *Make People Look Good*, expanded my vision of what was possible for me in my role as the center for the Utah Jazz. The outlet pass is one of the most crucial elements to the fast break in basketball and was something I excelled at. It is not a statistic that is tracked or noted. The outlet pass is thrown to the guard who runs down the court. That player generally hits a forward or guard with the ball enabling them to score. The guard passing the ball is credited with an assist, and the player scoring gets the points. I got the ball to my teammates and got the satisfaction of doing my job and moving my team closer to a win. Making my teammates look good made our team more successful.

Understand that every time you make the assist, every time you ask what you can do to help others, and every time you deliver on that promise, you'll not only make people look good, you'll shine as well.

QUESTIONS & EXERCISES

On a piece of paper or on your computer, write down the answers to the following questions.

- How focused are you on making others look good?

- On a scale from 1 to 10, how would you rate your effort to make others look good?

- What action steps can you take right now to improve that score?

- Who is someone you should acknowledge?

- How aware are you of the effect and impact your performance has on your team and teammates?

- Are there members of your team, family, or division who could use an "assist"? If so, what can you do to help them?

COMMITMENT #4

PROTECT OTHERS

CHAPTER 11

"A player that makes a team great is more valuable than a great player."

- JOHN WOODEN

WHEN YOU LOOK OUT for others and create
trust, you'll be amazed by what happens.
Almost without exception, they look out for
you in turn. When we elevate others, they elevate us. It can
manifest in different ways, but the core of Commitment #4
is always the same: ***Protect Others.***

Dave Checketts knows how to create trust and protect
others. He did it with the Jazz when he helped establish a
family dynamic among the members of a once-struggling
team. He did the same at the New York Knicks and Madison
Square Garden, when he helped transform the way the different departments and organizations looked out for each
other. And he helped instill a culture of trust and protec-
tion at another venture, Jet Blue Airways.

Back in 2000, Checketts was a founder of Jet Blue,
which marketed itself as a rival to low-fare leader Southwest
Airlines. Within its first year, the airline went from an inau-
gural flight to its one-millionth customer and $100 million

in flown revenue. The company has continued to grow since, and Checketts is still an owner, shareholder, and serves on the board of directors.

He said, "We set out to do something that had never been done, to return humanity back to air travel. It's hard to find and employ people who remain upbeat, who are customer-friendly, and who really want to solve your problems when a flight gets canceled. I think we've created a great culture, but it has not been easy. You do that by having policies that people actually value. And Jet Blue's employees did value these policies. They know their company has their backs. They know the company will do everything it can—despite otherwise catastrophic external factors—to ensure their job security."

Checketts protects his employees. He told me, "JetBlue started in 2000, and in 2001 the airline industry ran into enormous trouble when all flights were grounded for days and days after 9/11. Then the economic downturn of the late 2000s hit, and along with everyone else, we were in huge trouble. But throughout the turmoil, we never laid anyone off in terms of reducing the size of the company. In all this time, we've never furloughed anyone. We've always grown the company. We've remained independent. We've resisted all of the mergers to other airlines. As a result, we have a terrific culture. We've won eleven J.D. Power and Associates awards in a row for the best low-cost airline . . . eleven."

Who are you protecting? Who is protecting you?

It's 1986 and the Jazz are on the road to compete against

our archrival, the Portland Trailblazers. Head down, I pace back and forth across the lane beneath the basket of the Memorial Coliseum in Portland, Oregon. I am laser focused. I repeat my pre-game mantra, "This is my house." Three long strides, pivot, turn, back across the lane the other direction. "No one gets in here." I am completely determined. Completely focused. "This is my house. No one gets in here!"

The key, the lane, the paint—it is where I've honed my craft, where I've focused hours of training. It is where I "do my job." You come in from the left, I'm there.

You come in from the right, Big Mark is there.

This had been my pre-game ritual for eighty-two games a year since my career began. Without fail I prepared myself for every game this way. This particular game was one I will never forget.

From the opening tip, I made plays all over the court. I blocked shots, disrupted Portland's plays, grabbed rebounds, threw long outlet passes to John Stockton, who then passed to Karl Malone who scored easy goals at the other end of the floor.

It was like that all game long.

As the game wore on, the 14,000 fans in Memorial Coliseum grew silent. It's one of the greatest feelings you can experience in the NBA. There's nothing quite like *hearing* the impact you have on the other team.

We went on to win the game 95–90.

After the game, I went into the locker room and faced a familiar sight: Karl Malone surrounded by a crowd of reporters. He had an outstanding game and had scored 37 points that night.

The press doesn't really pay much attention to defensive players. So I showered, gathered my things, went back to the hotel, grabbed dinner, and went to bed. The next morning, I read the paper as I ate my breakfast.

A headline with my name jumped out and grabbed my attention, "Blazers just get Eaton up by the Jazz." The article started with quotes from the Trailblazers' coach that explained it wasn't Karl Malone they had so much trouble with, it was me! He went on to say that my defense was so disruptive that they couldn't run their plays; my performance was the deciding factor in the game.

In addition, I'd blocked *fourteen* shots, which was the third highest total for a game in the history of the NBA. And still is today.

On the court, my teammates knew they could take risks because they knew I had their back. They knew they could count on me. They could gamble more on defense because they knew if their man got by them, I would be there to help defend and ultimately block their shot. *I protected them.*

As I read the newspaper that day, it all came together for me. Everything my coaches had taught me made sense. My focus on my job, with precision and exactness, changed the outcome of the game. I made a difference. And you can too.

From the moment Wilt Chamberlain set me straight on what my job was as a basketball player, I dedicated myself to perfecting that role. In a sport that focuses on scoring and offensive statistics, my job was a role of service as a defender. My role was to be there for my teammates.

I was all right with that.

I marveled at the praise and credit I received from the Blazers' coach for my impact on the outcome of the game. I marveled because I was just doing my job: protecting the rim and my teammates.

WHEN I THINK ABOUT my time as a player and the coaches I played for, it's clear to me that I thrived and excelled in settings where I knew my coach had a plan for me and that he cared about me.

Coach Lubin believed in me long before I ever believed in myself. He showed me he cared from the start, when he picked me up for early morning practice.

As I transitioned from UCLA benchwarmer to an NBA starter, I wondered at the stark difference. I was the same player, the same person, possessing the same skill set. Why, *in just a few short months*, were the results so remarkably different?

The answer was clear. When I arrived at the Jazz, Coach Layden used the same approach with me as Coach Lubin. He believed in me. He had a plan for me, and he had a path for me to follow to maximize all that I could be.

Though they had radically different personalities, the common denominator between those two life-changing coaches was that they cared. They cared about me and about teaching me to do things the right way. They could see beyond the now, to the future of what I could become.

When people feel safe and cared for, they do their best. Imagine if, as managers, we showed our employees that we truly cared about them. If we viewed them as who they can become, not only as who they are right now.

Every time you help your department complete a project, every time you help your boss shine, every deadline you meet, you serve them. When you develop an ongoing commitment to service, you develop the habit of protecting others.

I talked with a client at Lincoln Financial Group, a Fortune 500 company. After speaking to some of their employee groups, I followed up with Garry Spence, vice president in the retirement plan services division, to get his take on the principle of protecting others.

Spence said protecting and serving others is so important to him and the company that he has given every individual in his organization a "challenge coin" as a reminder. On one side it reads, "Remember who you are and what you represent." On the other it says, "Make a meaningful impact on the lives of others through selfless service."

He explained, "This helps employees realize their job is not about them. It's not about making money. It's not about their commissions. It's not about their advancement. It's about making a meaningful impact in a person's life who trusts them enough to give them their retirement assets. Because when they sit down with us, our clients say, 'I'm scared. I'm fearful. I don't know if I can ever retire. I don't know if I'll make enough money.' They trust us."

Spence said his team has taken this mission of service very seriously and personally, saying, "The stories I hear are just remarkable, how our front-line advisors impact our clients' lives. They're willing to do things like meet a client at two or three in the morning, because the client works two jobs and only has time to meet while working the night shift at the second job."

This same mission of service has extended to how employees treat each other. Spence shared a story from his institutional sales team, a group that works with large companies. He brought on James as a sales representative. James was someone Spence had known at a previous company and whom he knew would give his all. James *did* give it his all, but for a variety of reasons, sales were not taking place in his region. Spence stepped in to do everything he could to help him, making sure he had base pay and any advances the company could give him, but it still wasn't enough to sustain James's family.

Spence described how another team member, Tim, saw James's struggle. Tim knew how hard it had to be for James; they both had a wife and five kids to provide for. Rather than sit idly by, Tim decided to do something. He invited James to work his cases with him and split the commissions on new plans until James got his territory going.

"It was the most beautiful thing to witness," said Spence. "James probably would not have been able to make it through that year had Tim not selflessly carved James into his compensation plan. He didn't have to do that, but he did."

The best part of the story is that the team hit their sales plan that year and James and Tim went on to meet or exceed their sales quotas year after year.

Just as Tim generously served James, there are rare companies that serve employees at that exalted level. In Chapter 6 I discussed Junior Bridgeman, who played for the Milwaukee Bucks and went on to become one of the nation's largest Wendy's franchise owners, employing over 20,000 people. Bridgeman has certainly demonstrated he knows a thing or two about business, but for him, the growth of the company and magnitude of its holdings are not his main focus. His focus and care are on the people who comprise his companies, Bridgeman Foods and the company's internal foundation, Manna.

Bridgeman takes a humble approach to management. He spent his first few years of ownership behind the counter at a franchise, flipping burgers and helping customers. He said, "One of the things that we really de-emphasize in our companies are titles. So when people would ask me if I'm the CEO or president, I'd say, 'No, I'm just the chief hamburger maker.' We all know our particular job: this is what I do, this is what you do, but avoiding title delineation has allowed us to be closer, to realize that we're all in this together."

That approach is embodied in Manna. The company invites every employee to donate at least one dollar from each paycheck, which goes into the foundation (many employees donate more).

Bridgeman explained, "The foundation is overseen by their fellow employees. If any employee has a tragedy or something happen to them, personally or within their family, they can ask the foundation for help. It can be a death in a family and the foundation takes care of the funeral, or any type of illness, or natural disaster. Their peers vote on the requests. When a request is granted, the money goes toward their situation. Even better, the employee does not have to pay the money back. This is a way for everybody in the company to help people going through tough times.

"I could tell you so many great stories of people who have been helped through difficulties. We helped an employee in Milwaukee whose apartment caught on fire and he lost everything. Another employee in Nashville had her husband leave her and her four kids. She couldn't pay the electric bill and was about to be evicted. Through Manna, our employees were able to help her get back on her feet."

Bridgeman has fostered a culture of service through the foundation and established a management culture at Bridgeman Foods that develops and trains employees. He said, "I think for us as a company, when we look back, if we didn't help someone become better—by better I mean become more proficient at their job which allowed them to move up the ladder, to make more money, and to help their family—if we didn't do that, then I think we will have failed. Because when it's all said and done, it's not about how many people we employed or how many restaurants we had or even how much money we made. If we can't look back and say we helped the lives of the people who came to work with us, then we have been a failure."

Wow, that is powerful!

That fierce loyalty is what distinguishes a team from a group, and loyalty develops from trust. Whether on a sports team, a business team, or in a personal relationship, trust is the foundation on which we build. Without it, a team or relationship will crumble.

The best teams I played on had that foundation of trust. It transformed us. Every player on our team protected every other player.

How do we develop that trust which is so critical to achieving success?

Trust comes when people know that you are there for them.

Trust comes when people know they can count on you.

Trust comes when people know you are committed to their well-being.

When you commit yourself to protecting others, you can expect an extraordinary commitment in return.

When you fight for someone else and transcend your self-interest, you change the world.

Doing more for others than we do for ourselves brings out the best in us.

If you want to be invaluable, be the person people can count on. If you want enduring relationships, look out for others; put them first.

I know this Commitment works, because I learned to do it well in the NBA. The things I did for my team did not always result in recognition for me, but it helped the Jazz win games and contributed to creating a viable, financially stable team. The payoff for me was a twelve-year career doing what I loved. It made me the person I am today and helped me go on to success in other fields.

Look at your life and career. Are you someone who empowers your colleagues and boss? Are you showing up for others? Are you willing to do what it takes to protect others?

If you can answer yes to all of those questions, you're on your way to being an All-Star player on an All-Star team. A place where you have a supreme sense of satisfaction, of mattering, and of helping others reach success.

CHAPTER 12

"The most important measure of how good a game I played was how much better I'd made my teammates play."

- BILL RUSSELL

I T IS MUCH EASIER to do a job well when we feel our coach or boss cares about us and has our back. From the start, I knew Coach Layden cared about my teammates and me. It was important to him that our team learned to care for others as well. He was famous for pulling players aside and asking, "Have you called your Mom lately?" or "When is the last time you called your high school or college coach?" He bought books for players when we were on the road and encouraged us to read.

Frank Layden knew a powerful secret. He understood his role was much bigger than the numbers that showed up in the win-loss column, ticket sales, and financial reports. He knew that when he cared for and protected us, and taught us to do the same, the material things—wins, financial success, and increased ticket sales—would come.

The simple but important principle Coach Layden imparted was this: "It's not all about you! You didn't get here because you were singularly fantastic. You got to where you are with the help of the people around you—your family, your coaches, a friend, your teammates. Honor that. Put your focus back on them."

One of the best ways I know to do this is to see everything you do as an opportunity to serve others. I promise you this is a life-altering paradigm shift. When I was on the court, every time I blocked a shot, every time I got a defensive rebound and passed the ball to one of my teammates to take down the court, was a chance to serve and protect my teammates, to help my team win.

Sometimes, protecting others can require us to do more than we expected. It can also solidify relationships and show people we care. One such incident is forever etched in my mind. It is one time in many that Coach Layden showed just how deeply he cared for each member of our team.

We acquired John Drew in the earlier mentioned Dominique Wilkins trade. Drew was a prolific scorer and a great addition to our team on the court. Off the court, however, he had struggled for years with substance abuse.

We were in the middle of a grueling twelve-day road trip. After playing a game in Atlanta, we flew to Cleveland, where we had a two-day layover. Upon arriving in Cleveland, we realized that Drew wasn't with the team. Our trainer, Don "Sparky" Sparks, always made it a point to have contacts who apprised him of shady characters who hung around our team. Once they realized Drew was missing, Sparky immediately sought out some of his contacts. They determined Drew was still in Atlanta, at a crack house.

Coach Layden and Sparky did what they would have done for their own sons. They immediately jumped on a plane and flew back to Atlanta. Upon arriving there, Coach Layden hired a bodyguard and set out for the crack house, which was located in one of the most dangerous areas of the city. Just as Sparky had been informed, Drew was inside and was not in good shape. Coach Layden and Sparky retrieved him. They got him on a plane and checked him into a rehabilitation facility.

This story will never cease to touch and amaze me. It is the epitome of Commitment #4, **Protect Others**. It is incredible to me that Coach Layden and Sparky cared enough about one of their players to put their lives at risk to get him out of a bad situation, but it doesn't surprise me that these two men did so.

WHEN I WAS DRAFTED by the Jazz there were twenty-eight teams in the NBA. On average, every off season each team would usually have two roster spots to fill, for a grand total of only fifty-six available spots per year in the entire NBA. With 351 Division I college basketball teams in the country, hundreds of lower division teams, and hundreds more international players, there were literally thousands of players vying for just fifty-six spots. (Today there are thirty teams, and sixty spots.) Statistics show that only 3 in 10,000 high school seniors, or 0.03 percent, get drafted into the NBA. You have approximately the same chance of getting struck by lightning in your lifetime as being drafted by an NBA team. To say the odds of a college basketball player making an NBA roster are very slim is an understatement. To make a team is to be the elite of the elite.

I faced these odds, knowing I had already been struck by lightning when I was drafted. I was determined to make the most of my opportunity. I believed that if I continued to be dedicated and work out, I would secure one of those coveted roster spots. So, when Coach Layden asked me to come a month early to work on my game, I jumped at the chance.

Coach Layden had brought in assistant coach Phil Johnson to work with me. He helped me with my skills, my endurance, and taught me what it was like to be a professional basketball player. I was extremely grateful that I arrived in Utah early, since I quickly learned that I wasn't prepared for the level of conditioning required to play in the NBA.

I was committed to improvement, and Jazz Coach Phil Johnson was committed to me. From the beginning, he focused on the basics. He said, "Let's really work on conditioning, on the little things." I practiced all the fundamental basketball moves most people learned in high school. Up until this point, outside of working with Coach Lubin, I hadn't received individual coaching. I had never been exposed to many of the things Johnson showed me. His coaching and the work we did together boosted my confidence. I began to feel more comfortable with the ball out on the floor. The conditioning drills put me in the best shape I had ever been in.

I'm sure the coaches had their doubts about me the first few weeks, but through my hard work and determination I slowly began to improve. The key to my improvement was not only my industriousness and resolve; it was also the belief the Jazz coaches had in me. They knew it would take time for me to develop, and they were patient, letting me develop and make mistakes along the way. They protected me.

Coach Layden understood the importance of patience and creating an environment where each player could improve as an individual, and we could improve as a team. He was most concerned with long-term results.

This approach is not typical in professional basketball. Most coaches and management pull a player if they struggle during consecutive plays, let alone a few games. I was privileged to have a coaching staff who genuinely cared about my personal progress and saw my potential.

We often hear the phrase, "Failure is not an option." In my opinion and experience, both on and off the court, failure is not only an option, it is inevitable, because perfection is not attainable. Some form of failure is a reality and, in fact, desirable because we learn from our mistakes. It is difficult to even say the word failure, isn't it? So how do we handle the gap between the expectation that we must always succeed and the reality that we'll often fail?

Realizing that failure is a natural part of the growth process is crucial. It's how we developed as kids (as anyone who has witnessed a toddler transition from crawling to walking can attest). It's how we learned in school. And for professional athletes, it's a part of every practice, every drill, and every game. The biggest difference is that we often fail in front of tens of thousands of fans, millions of TV viewers, countless reporters, and social media critics.

I had to learn powerful strategies to shut out negative voices (the ones in my own head, as well as those of the fans and reporters) and allow myself to experience the necessary learning curve everyone faces. I also discovered the benefits and advantages of being part of a team who made room for each other's mistakes, and who always had each other's backs.

Learning how to handle failure is critical to your individual success and that of your team. Because, like it or not, setbacks are part of the process. If you haven't already, you will likely say something wrong in a meeting. You'll miss a deadline. You'll be off the mark when your part of a project is delivered. You'll disappoint a client. Welcome to being human.

The key is to stay focused on the end goal, and to keep going. It's not important that you dropped the ball. It's important that you picked it up, kept going, and learned how to handle the ball better next time.

And if you're not the one who made the mistake (this time) be there to provide understanding and support for your colleague, spouse, or boss when they err.

If you're in management, it's just as vital—if not more so—to communicate to your employees that you understand when they make a few blunders, and that you're there to back them up while they solve them. This was something Coach Layden made possible for me and the other players on our team—and it's something that can make a difference for your team, as well.

When I sat down with Mountain America Credit Union

CEO Sterling Nielsen, he said, "We create a safe environment where it's okay to make a mistake. There's a fine line between a mistake and incompetence; making a mistake is okay. We create an environment where employees can experiment, where they can go out and do the best they know how. We also provide resources for them to learn and grow and develop new skills so they can be prepared for the next challenge. We've found this to be very successful in moving things forward."

Accepting failure, turning it into a learning experience, and supporting others as they do the same is a powerful part of Commitment #4—*Protect Others*.

The Utah Jazz organization has been a standard-bearer for consistency and stability. From long-time owner Larry Miller to the guy selling popcorn at the stadium, the Jazz has made loyalty one of its hallmarks. This commitment to stability from the front office has allowed the coaches to feel secure and confident in doing their jobs. They know that management will have their backs even if the win doesn't always show on the scoreboard. It gives players confidence in the organization and the system—they know that even if they aren't playing their best at any given moment, the organization sees the big picture and takes the long view. This also spills over into the community. The fans trust that the team expects to maintain a certain level of excellence and will do whatever it takes to earn the crowd's support.

In a league known for constant turnover in the coaching ranks, the Jazz have had just five coaches since moving to Salt Lake City in 1979. That is unheard of in professional sports. That shows loyalty. That shows commitment.

As of this book's publication, the most successful Utah Jazz coach is Jerry Sloan. Sloan coached the Jazz for 22 seasons from 1989 to 2011. I had the privilege of playing for Coach Sloan for six years. He is the third-most winning coach in NBA history. He won 1,221 games throughout his career; 1,127 with the Jazz. He also holds the record for the most consecutive games coached with the same team in NBA history. In an industry famous for hiring and firing on a whim, Coach Sloan built an unbelievable legacy of loyalty and consistency, which made him one of the greatest coaches in the NBA. It's why he was inducted into the Naismith Basketball Hall of Fame.

I asked Coach Sloan what he felt the biggest contributing factor was to the Jazz's success, what made our team what it was, and what gave us such a great chance of winning night after night.

His answer might surprise you. He didn't say it was great players. He didn't say it was great coaching. He said, "It started from the top of the organization, all the way down. I could tell our players when they came in the fall to start the season, 'I'm going to be here no matter what, and you may not be. Players are expendable, but I am going to be here.'"

He went on to explain how much it meant to him that the Jazz owner, Larry Miller, and the front office always had his back. Coach Sloan felt confident that his job was safe, that he would have the constant support of management and ownership. This allowed him to do his job and build a group of players who truly functioned as a team. The attitude of teamwork and protecting others that Larry Miller instilled led the Jazz to back-to-back NBA Finals appearances. The legacy of support from management has made the Utah Jazz one of the most admired sports franchises in the country.

The culture of stability and success created by the Utah Jazz paid off through the '80s, '90s, and beyond. However, it wasn't always that way. It is no secret that during the early years, in the mid-'70s, the Jazz struggled financially. When Frank Layden was hired as general manager in '79, the team's last year in New Orleans, times were extremely tough. The move to Utah didn't make things any easier. Instability and financial stress contributed to high turnover in staff. During the '80–'81 season the team traded nearly fifty players, and management was a revolving door. Later in 1981, when owner Sam Battistone asked Layden to do double-time as general manager and head coach, the team could only offer him a two-year coaching contract.

Layden, however, understood the importance of stability. He proposed they announce his appointment as a ten-year, one-million-dollar coaching contract. The news was well received, and the players and fans started to buy into the long-term vision he and the management had for the team.

Just a few years later, Dave Checketts joined the team as president and general manager. It was his first role in the NBA and he wanted in-depth knowledge on what it would take for the team to improve.

Management commissioned a study on what makes a great franchise versus a franchise that always struggles. "The biggest factor was stability," said Checketts. "Stability in the front office, stability in ownership, and especially stability in basketball operations. Players needed to know whom they played for. They needed to know that the coaches were safe, and that we weren't making changes just because players may not like them."

Together, Checketts and Layden reinforced that environment as much as possible and that approach continued for decades, with good results.

Establishing an environment of loyalty and stability is important to your team, family, business, and your community. Sowing seeds of trustworthiness and allegiance with even the most vulnerable members of society reaps benefits for all. I learned that in a very personal and significant way when I started the non-profit organization Standing Tall for Youth and ran it for thirteen years. Standing Tall for Youth provided opportunities for at-risk youth to participate in basketball camps, outdoor activities, and team-building exercises year round.

One of the most memorable success stories from that endeavor involved a young woman named Kandyce. We started working with her when she was about eleven years old. She came to us as a tough street kid who had been through a lot, but was willing to work hard. She was a staff favorite, and camp MVP five or six years in a row. Several years after she moved on from our organization, I got a Facebook friend request from her. After I accepted the request, she sent me a message. It was a picture of her master's degree in social work from the University of Utah! Incorporating the Four Commitments in your life in a way that pays it forward is not only personally rewarding, it also creates a better world. Kandyce is now paying forward the lessons, experiences, and opportunities she received and is having a positive impact on the lives of many other young people. The stability and support provided by our program played a significant role in her achievements.

In any workplace, stability is a critical ingredient in overall success. It is another aspect to protecting others. When employees feel secure in company objectives, management, and work groups, they are confident of their place in the company's future and motivated to contribute to that future.

As an individual, you can contribute to an atmosphere of stability by making your family, friends, and co-workers feel safe, supported, and protected. Avoid doing things that contribute to internal conflict like gossiping, backstabbing, and being hypercritical.

Likewise, managers and supervisors can produce and maintain an environment of stability. Instead of churning through front-line workers, develop employees through training and constructive feedback so they can move up in the ranks.

The restaurant business is notorious for high employee turnover rates. However, I have seen firsthand at our restaurants, Tuscany and Franck's, the impact stability and support can have on employees. We have chefs, servers, and managers who have been with us for a dozen years or more.

There are a few contributing factors to our stability and the loyalty it inspires. First, we empower our staff by letting them have a voice in decision-making. They know they are part of a team. We are all there to create an excellent dining experience for our customers. We give our employees the tools to do their job, proper server and culinary training and wine education, and we expect them to excel in the execution of those jobs, whether it's service, cooking, beverage service, or managing the front of the house. The result is that our customers want to return, and the restaurants are successful.

Second, we adopted the team philosophy with my original restaurant partner, Aaron Ferer. Ferer owned several restaurants in San Francisco, one of the nation's most competitive markets. He learned the best way to succeed in the restaurant business is to have great reviews. The only way to maintain continued great reviews is to give diners a consistent experience, day in and day out. That means great food, great service, and a great atmosphere, with a commitment to excellence that never wavers.

And finally, we focused on the little things, like acknowledging customers by name; knowing who likes their martini with three olives, not one, and who likes to have coffee after dessert; offering a creative menu; and giving people an enjoyable dining experience every time.

Just like a restaurant, where you're only as good as your last happy customer, your company is only as good as your last employee, product, presentation, or service. You maintain success by maintaining excellence, which is maintained by stability, which is attained by protecting each other.

There is another aspect of protecting others that can best be summarized with one word: family. When we treat people like treasured family members miracles happen.

David Stern, the former NBA Commissioner who helped transform the league from a largely ignored American sport to the worldwide phenomenon it is today, concurs. He attributes much of his success to the sense of family he fostered and created among the NBA home office staff. As that staff grew from 24 employees to 1,200 employees, the family atmosphere grew too.

Stern explained, "Our people knew it, they absolutely came to accept and embrace heartily that we were there to work very hard, but that we would always protect each other. Our short phrase was *Work and play well with others*. We called it the NBA family, and we abided by that notion of family in every way. Whether it was our family's joys or tragedies—we shared it all. We became an extraordinary network. If anyone in our organization ever had a medical problem, I would use my board service in various organizations to help. I laugh now, but I essentially became the largest doctor referral service around, because no matter where you were in the organization, if you had a problem, you knocked on my door. I had an open-door policy, and I would help make sure everyone got the care they needed."

Stern made it his business to make his employees feel noticed and valued. He said, "I used to thank all of our receptionists, because I knew they were the face of our company. I had people say to me, 'Boy, I love so-and-so because she's always smiling. She always greets me and remembers me." The people on the front lines who interact with consumers or the public are your first line of developing people's impression of you. So take care of them."

Many successful businesses have employed this family approach. My head coach at Cypress College, Don Johnson, played for revered Coach John Wooden in the early '50s, and said Wooden treated each of his players like a son. He recalled, "Coach Wooden helped me get summer jobs at UCLA. He helped me get my apartment. My graduate year there, I became pretty sick on a Sunday. He was over there within ten minutes to help. I was not special in any area; I was just a human being who played for him. Now multiply that times hundreds and hundreds of kids who have played for him—he would pay equal attention to all of us."

Johnson said Wooden's kindness did not stop when he graduated. Wooden was in attendance when Johnson's high school inducted him into its Hall of Fame. Wooden also cheered Johnson on at his retirement celebration. Wooden won ten NCAA championships—seven of them in consecutive years (no other team has won more than two in a row). He was a basketball legend, but he didn't consider himself great. He considered himself part of a family, a family he diligently nurtured year in and year out.

On a recent trip to Wisconsin, I saw the concept of colleagues as family in action. I arrived at Lambeau Field, home of the NFL's beloved Green Bay Packers, to give a speech in a conference center at the football complex.

I was able to tour the stadium, and as I walked the

hallowed halls of this revered space, it was evident in every step I took that I was in a home. In that home, they honored and paid homage to their ancestors. I strolled by a plaque with the team history, which highlighted the fact the Packers are a community-owned team. I strode through the locker room and players' meeting rooms, and imagined I was in the large family room of very proud parents. There were photos on the walls of past players, and each room was named after a former Packer. There is no doubt in my mind the members of that team felt a deep loyalty and obligation to their "family." As a Green Bay Packer, there is a clear cultural expectation of excellence implied before you ever step foot on the field.

To feel connected to those around you and work jointly toward something bigger than yourself inspires success. The more a company feels familial, the more likely people are to remain committed and contribute to the growth of the company. When employees treat each other with respect and care, the company flourishes. The more management treats employees as integral members of the team, the more the company thrives. Why? Because they feel valued at a deep level. They feel like they matter. They feel like what they have to offer makes a difference.

This sense of family doesn't have to start at the top. It can come from the employees and travel upward as well. I know this because I've spent several years in management, and I've personally been touched by kind words and gestures from our staff. They have made me feel valued and inspired *me* to extend that concern and care to them. It is a contagious circle of giving, which enhances the spirit of teamwork.

Write your boss a note. Get him an unexpected cup of coffee. Help her meet her quotas or deadlines, congratulate her on the promotion. Not only will it make you both feel great, but there's also credibility to the old adage: If you want to get promoted, help your boss get promoted!

Every time I stepped on the court, I made my dedication to Commitment #4, *Protect Others,* clear. I was conscious that one of my primary goals was to protect my teammates. That meant claiming the key as my house, and doing everything I could to keep the opposition from scoring in that house.

By protecting others, I led the league in blocked shots four of my eleven seasons, was a five-time member on the NBA All Defensive team, and twice named NBA Defensive Player of the Year. I hold two NBA records: most blocked shots in one season (456) and career average blocked shots (3.5.) That is the impact Commitment #4 had in ways that are easily quantified. The impact was much greater than stats alone demonstrate, however.

To get a good idea of the influence my contribution had, look at the shooting percentages of opposing teams and players when I was in the game. They altered shots and altered strategies when they faced our team. The average number of points scored against our team dropped dramatically when I focused on protecting my teammates.

You, too, may have to look deeper to find what your true impact is when you align yourself with Commitment #4 and protect others.

When you implement Commitment #4 and **Protect Others**, you can create a stable environment where people feel protected, where they are cared for, and where they are treated like family. When trust is fostered, personal and professional growth is encouraged, and allowances are made for mistakes, people excel and relationships thrive!

QUESTIONS & EXERCISES

On a piece of paper or on your computer, write down the answers to the following questions.

- How focused are you on protecting others?

- On a scale from 1 to 10, how would you rate your effort in protecting others?

- What action can you take right now to improve your score?

- Name three people you need to let know you have their back.

- What can you do to foster loyalty and create a family feeling on your team?

CHAPTER 13

"Get the fundamentals down and the level of everything you do will rise."

- MICHAEL JORDAN

W HEN I THINK BACK on the days Coach Lubin coaxed me onto the court for a few hours, I remember how awkward I was at first: my clumsy grip on the ball; my legs so tight from years bending over engines I could hardly move. I imagine what it must have been like for someone to watch me learn the basics that had always eluded me. I am grateful beyond words my coach saw through those deficits to my true potential.

Among the many significant lessons taught by my mentors, among whom I include Tom Lubin, Wilt Chamberlain, Frank Layden, and Jerry Sloan, one of the most powerful was the value of fundamentals.

NBA Hall of Famer Rick Barry and I recently discussed how the fundamentals of basketball are the foundation for a long career in the game. He said that like skyscrapers, we need a strong foundation for any kind of success.

Skyscrapers are remarkable feats of engineering. Before the mass production of steel, no one built anything higher than ten stories—wood and brick just weren't enough to support a building any taller. Today, the tallest buildings in the world, like Burj Khalifa in Dubai and Shanghai Tower in China, draw our eyes up over 2,000 feet high.

What's beneath those skyscrapers, though, is just as remarkable.

For a skyscraper to defy gravity, wind, and seismic activity it needs a solid foundation. Before the floors of a building can climb into the atmosphere, crews must dig several stories deep into the earth. There they create a foundation sturdy enough for story after story of steel beams, concrete, and glass to ascend.

Like a skyscraper, a solid foundation in the fundamentals of basketball can take one to great heights. Barry explained that his dad, who had coached him throughout his childhood, was big on fundamentals. He would have Barry and his older brother run drill after drill, until things like dribbling the ball without looking and the correct way to box out were second nature. "He told me if I wanted to be a good player, I needed to learn how to do these things. And if I ignored the basics during a game, I'd find myself sitting next to him on the bench. Not for mistakes like a missed shot, but if I did something that was fundamentally unsound, he'd pull me and have me think about it," said Barry.

Barry went on to play for the University of Miami and was drafted to the Warriors in the mid-'60s. He became an offensive icon, a twelve-time NBA All-Star who scored more than 25,000 points in fourteen seasons. He said the fundamentals his dad taught him were instrumental to that success. "It served me, because as other coaches came in to teach new things, it was easy to pick them up because I already had the foundation to build on. In basketball, even if you're incredibly gifted and have natural abilities, you're only going to go so far, and then that building topples over without the foundation."

The Four Commitments of a Winning Team provides a foundation on which you and your team can build. Like the skyscraper's foundation, the Four Commitments will help you, your organization, and your family build to heights you never imagined possible.

Let's briefly revisit *The Four Commitments of a Winning Team*:

KNOW YOUR JOB

I executed the fundamentals Coach Lubin and Wilt Chamberlain taught me. I learned and embraced my job, and went from benchwarmer to All-Star.

DO WHAT YOU'RE ASKED TO DO

I did exactly what Coach Layden asked me to when I was a rookie. He gave me a training regimen to follow, assigned me grueling daylong workouts with coaches, and I committed to do exactly what he asked.

MAKE OTHERS LOOK GOOD

I accepted my role as a big man. I didn't begrudge the fame of players like Stockton and Malone, who got the lion's share of media attention. I helped them look good. That led me to being named NBA Defensive Player of the Year, twice.

PROTECT OTHERS

I protected the basket, blocked shots, grabbed rebounds, and passed the ball. I led the league in blocked shots four separate seasons and became a defensive force for which opposing coaches had to adjust their game plan. I protected my teammates, which led me to an NBA All-Star game.

WHEN I COMMITTED to the fundamentals and embraced the value of teamwork my basketball career skyrocketed. That perspective laid the foundation for me to develop skills, take on new challenges, and build a life that took off in ways I could never have imagined.

Dave Checketts agreed with me that a shared vision of teamwork is essential. He said, "Teamwork really starts with getting buy-in from everybody who's on the floor, in the front office, or in the company. It starts with coming together to ask, 'What is the vision? What are we trying to accomplish? How can we make it happen?' And it's creating that vision that people, then, either buy into, or they don't."

Checketts said he learned a lot from his early days at the Jazz. He noted that the Jazz players who never accepted the team vision, those who played for themselves first and team second, didn't stick around long. As Frank Layden and the management team put together a group of players who *did* embrace that vision of teamwork, the Jazz record began to change. We went on to become one of the best teams in the league.

When Checketts moved to the Knicks and Madison Square Garden, he brought with him the concept of teamwork he'd learned at the Jazz. In fact, it became a key trait he looked for when he hired anyone.

"We changed our recruiting practices and our interview process," he told me. "Our whole appraisal process revolved around identifying whether people would be a cultural fit for us, whether they felt like team mattered more to them than their own individual success."

I recommend adopting a similar approach if you hire employees. If you have candidates with similar qualifications and experience, make it a priority to hire the employee with a solid foundation and commitment to teamwork.

And if you want to make a difference as an employee, to improve your company's bottom line (and your own), become the team player who makes themselves invaluable to your boss. Share in the vision of teamwork and incorporate the Four Commitments in your everyday approach to work.

I am a living testament that embracing the Four Commitments pays off. As I work with top-tier companies across the nation, and run businesses of my own, I can attest that teamwork is a major factor in the success of any person or organization.

John Wooden sums it up perfectly, "A player that makes his team great is more valuable than a great player." My life has benefited from this perspective, and I've seen countless other lives elevated by this belief as well.

The Four Commitments—knowing my job, doing what

was asked, making people look good, and protecting my teammates—made me a valuable player. My value came from making my team great. When my contributions combined with those of my committed teammates and the Jazz staff, we went from a ranking at the bottom of the league, with a record of thirty wins and fifty-two losses, to *division champions* the following year with a record of forty-five wins and thirty-seven losses. We made it to the playoffs for the first time in franchise history, and continued to make the NBA playoffs for the next twenty seasons consecutively.

In my second season, four of the eight NBA statistical leaders for the season were Utah Jazz players. In the seventy-one seasons in NBA history, that is the *only* time that has happened. And this came just one year after being ranked at the bottom of the league. That team was a direct result of players who were dedicated to the Four Commitments, and being part of that team is one of my greatest accomplishments.

When I recount everything I gained from my career in the NBA—the financial rewards, the lessons learned, and accolades received—the most valuable thing I acquired was the knowledge of the effectiveness and power that comes with incorporating the Four Commitments in every area of my life. They have always led me to success.

Allow the Four Commitments to guide you to success. Be a team player. Help your team win. As your colleagues, boss, employees, family, and friends score in life, you will find *yourself* the winner.

Share the Four Commitments with the people you value most—your family, colleagues, and friends. When each of you embrace the Commitments you will see miracles. It's simple; to win, help others win. That is what life is all about. If we look back on our lives, most of us were happiest when we helped someone else. If you want to be happy, commit yourself to others and the rest will come.

ACKNOWLEDGMENTS

Writing your first book is a big step into the unknown. Like most challenging and worthwhile things, it was accomplished with an All-Star team assisting me. First, to my wife Teri, thank you for your love and unwavering belief in me. Teri helped me take on this project, which had been put on the shelf, and drive it to the finish line. My deepest gratitude and love go to her. Her passion for my message and her relentless perseverance to gather the right people and resources to create something special is the reason you are holding this book in your hands today.

To my dad, Budd Eaton, thank you for teaching me the value of hard work, healthy living, and instilling a desire for life-long learning. To my coach Lisa Yakobi, with whom I co-wrote my Four Commitments keynote presentation, thank you for taking me deeper than I wanted to go. To Stacy Dymalski, my thanks for your valuable insight that kept our writing on track. To Steve and Heather Beers, thank you for getting us started and creating the framework of the manuscript. To my editor, Sydny Miner, and book designer, Francine Platt, all I can say is, wow, am I happy to have you on my team. To Justin Branch and the great team at Greenleaf Book Group, thank you for your guidance as we pulled this book together.

My gratitude and thanks to my good friend and prolific best-selling author, Richard Paul Evans, who took this rookie under his wing and showed me how the Big Boys do it! Thank you for your insight, wisdom, and willingness to walk alongside me.

To my former and current restaurant partners, Aaron Ferer and Guy Wadsworth, thank you for teaching me how to run a results-driven business and for your commitment to excellence and execution.

To my coaches and teammates, thank you for making me a better player and person.

ABOUT THE AUTHOR

M ARK EATON is a 7'4" NBA All-Star, motivational speaker, entrepreneur, and author. He is passionate about sharing his teamwork message and has spoken to many world-class organizations, including IBM, FedEx, Phillips 66, Caesars Entertainment, HEAD USA, Big O Tires, TD Ameritrade, Farmers Insurance, T-Mobile, Habitat for Humanity, and LG—as well as businesses, government agencies, and universities at every level. He has been featured as a team building expert in print and online publications such as Forbes.com, *Sports Illustrated*, and Entreprenuer.com.

In addition to his work on team building, Eaton is managing partner in two award-winning restaurants in Salt Lake City, Tuscany and Franck's, recently voted Best Restaurant in Utah.

He is also founder and former chairman of the Mark Eaton Standing Tall for Youth Foundation, which provided sports and outdoor opportunities for more than 3,000 at-risk children. He is a former president and board member of the Legends of Basketball, which supports the needs of retired NBA players. He attended Cypress College and the University of California, Los Angeles (UCLA).

Eaton's radio and television experience includes eight years hosting Jazz Tonight on KJZZ-TV, host of Mark Eaton Outdoors on The Outdoor Channel, and three-year host of Sports Health Today, an internationally syndicated radio show.

When Mark is not speaking, writing, or working he enjoys traveling with his wife Teri, horseback riding, mountain biking, skiing, and the outdoors. He lives in Park City, Utah with his wife, children, horses, dogs, and barn cats.

For more information about the author, visit www.7ft4.com.